LUCIEN MAXWELL
Villain or Visionary

Harriet Freiberger

LUCIEN MAXWELL

Villain or Visionary

SUNSTONE
PRESS

SANTA FE

Line Drawings by Jean Kashner

Portrait of Lucien Maxwell
courtesy of the Philmont Museum, Cimarron, New Mexico

Sunstone books may be purchased for educational, business, or sales promotional use. For information please write: Special Markets Department, Sunstone Press, P.O. Box 2321, Santa Fe, New Mexico 87504-2321.

FIRST EDITION

10 9 8 7 6 5 4 3 2 1

Library of Congress Cataloging in Publication Data:
Freiberger, Harriet, 1938–
    Lucien Maxwell: villain or visionary / by Harriet Freiberger. —
1st ed.
        p. cm.
    includes bibliographical references and index.
    ISBN: 0-86534-286-5
    1. Maxwell, Lucien Bonaparte, 1818–1875. 2. Pioneers — New Mexico — Biography. 3. Ranchers — New Mexico — Biography. 4. Landowners — New Mexico — Biography. 5. New Mexico — History — 1848- 6. Cimarron (N.M.) — Biography. I. Title.
F801.M39F74   1999
978.9′ 04′ 092 — dc21
[B]   99–10210
                          CIP

Published by   SUNSTONE PRESS
                    Post Office Box 2321
                    Santa Fe, NM 87504-2321 / USA
                    (505) 988-4418 / *orders only* (800) 243-5644
                    FAX (505) 988-1025

FOR MY HEROES, FRY AND LUCIEN

CONTENTS

LIST OF ILLUSTRATIONS

Lucien Maxwell. Courtesy Philmont Museum, Cimarron, New Mexico.

A LETTER TO THE READER

Ten years ago, when I visited northeastern New Mexico for the first time, I heard jokes about a twenty-three-year-old mountain man who married thirteen-year-old Luz Beaubien, a girl so ugly, they said, that on the day of her wedding she wore a black veil over her face. Deriding the accomplishments of Lucien Maxwell, who, according to legend, was the largest single owner of land in the United States, they said he married to obtain his father-in-law's wealth.

No one seemed to think anything good about the man who was so much a part of New Mexico's territorial history. Lucien Maxwell was rich, I heard, so rich that he kept bars of gold in his desk drawer; so rich that he entertained everyone who traveled the mountain branch of the Santa Fe Trail in his palatial mansion; so rich that he could afford to live in the lap of luxury when all around him Indians and Mexicans starved.

In 1870, at the age of fifty-one, after building his "empire" for twenty years, this "land baron" sold out, exchanged his land for cash, and left the Cimarron country. He had paid fifty thousand dollars for the land and an undetermined amount for the vast improvements he had made thereon. He walked away with six hundred and fifty thousand.

With an intensity that defies reason, something drew me to Lucien Maxwell's defense. Why would someone sell out and leave, leave the land he had risked everything to cultivate? As I read and researched and followed where his footsteps had been, I began taking the side of Lucien Maxwell. I am convinced that he deserves recognition for his leadership in developing what was then the New Mexico Territory.

Separating fact from fiction, I discovered that Luz Beaubien was actually a beautiful young woman, that the only picture of her was taken when she was elderly and quite heavy. I learned that Luz's father was indeed wealthy, owner of two large Mexican land grants in what is now northern New Mexico and southern Colorado; but Lucien Maxwell purchased his interests in the Beaubien and Miranda Grant, gaining by inheritance with Luz only a one-eighteenth interest. As for his being the largest single land owner in the United States, Lucien shared ownership of the grant with his wife. And, New Mexican attorney Thomas Catron's holdings far exceeded Lucien's, Catron having had during his lifetime an interest in at least thirty-four land grants and controlling interest in over three million acres of land. Most important of all, I learned that the government could have purchased Maxwell's land for an Indian reservation, even after gold was discovered there, for only two hundred fifty thousand dollars.

Too much evidence painted a picture entirely different from a land-grabbing opportunist. Too many stories survived about his good nature and generosity. Lucien Maxwell lived at a time and in a place where his very life depended upon every decision. Mistakes in judgement cost far more than gold.

Perhaps our modern culture cannot understand what it means to be self-reliant. Perhaps I have been caught up in romantic idealism. Or maybe I recognize in Lucien Maxwell a human being who earned the right to live. Either way, he has earned my respect.

Now, whenever I drive south from Denver, I'm aware of his footsteps across the road I'm traveling, from Bent's Fort westward toward Spanish Peaks and then south into New Mexico. Atop Raton Pass, I stop and look out over the high plains abutting snow-covered mountains to the west. He, too, must have stood below Fisher's Peak, savoring the scent of pine, becoming part of endless, cloudless blue sky. If I concentrate, hear only the sound of the wind and feel only the warmth of the sun, I can turn to see a dark-haired man astride his horse, his blue eyes smiling at me from beneath his hat's slouching brim, his hand raised in greeting.

"It was everything you have imagined," he acknowledges my thoughts in a pleasantly deep voice, "and I welcome you to my Cimarron country."

Harriet Freiberger

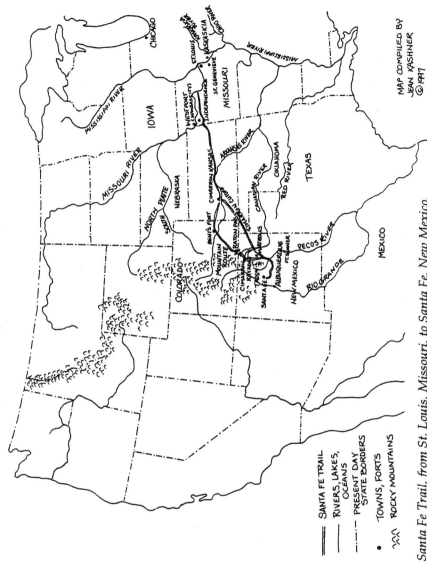

Santa Fe Trail, from St. Louis, Missouri, to Santa Fe, New Mexico.

INTRODUCTION

Three quarters of a century is a long time to remember an unmarked grave, but Lucien Maxwell's life was its own memorial. For two decades he built on land granted by Mexico's governor long before New Mexico became a state. He farmed, ranched, and traded where a thousand miles and a two-month journey separated western outposts from Saint Louis and "civilization."

Through his efforts a town grew, a town where, for the most part, people were happy and could live without fear, where strangers were welcome and travelers on the Santa Fe Trail partook of his hospitality. In a place and time when lawlessness was the rule, he proved himself capable of maintaining order, nurturing the future of the territory that would become the forty-seventh state. Everyone who traveled the mountain route knew the name of Lucien Maxwell. All were welcomed into his home, for a meal and a night's rest under a roof.

Hundreds of American Indians, Mexicans, and Anglos thrived under his leadership. Only after most of them died did the need for a marker at his grave site occur to anyone. Even now, one hundred twenty-four years after his death, the stories continue to be told about the man who left more than a physical imprint upon New Mexico, the man who welcomed into his home and at his overflowing dinner table Indian, Mexican, and Anglo; soldier, trader, and preacher; rich, poor, stranger, and friend.

Detractors called Lucien's Cimarron country an empire. Admirers saw it as a barony. Travelers on the Santa Fe Trail welcomed it as a godsend. Historians admit it was a successful, self-sustaining community. Lucien and Luz Maxwell called it home.

A multiplicity of traditions and cultures merged into that home, destiny having brought together in this couple the disparate elements brimming to the top of United States western expansion. By the time twenty-three-year-old Lucien met and married Luz, he could already converse fluently in Spanish, French, and various Indian languages. When the rest of the country was hurrying in search of gold, first to California then to Colorado, and later to Nevada, Lucien Maxwell and his friend Kit Carson decided to call New Mexico home. They had both married young, Mexican brides before taking off together on expeditions with explorer John Frémont. Even the invitation of John Frémont to join him in California failed to dissuade the famous Indian scout from "settling down" with his friend Lucien on the eastern side of the Sangre de Cristo Mountains.

Twenty increasingly successful years passed during which Lucien and Luz acquired not only great wealth but also total ownership of the one million seven hundred thousand-acre Beaubien and Miranda Land Grant. Then, at the age of fifty-one, Lucien Maxwell sold out and left the Cimarron country.

Some say that "Mac" was taken advantage of by faster-thinking speculators, in the sale of the grant and in later investments. Others accuse him of greedy speculation. Some say he married Luz Beaubien to gain the Mexican Land Grants held by her father, *rico* of Taos. Others say he had a "good head" for business and was of inestimable value to his father-in-law after Luz's brother Narciso was killed during the Taos Rebellion. Some say he "controlled" his peons and Indians with harsh discipline; others say he maintained peace and prosperity in the community he built. Attitudes and perspectives differed, but in 1865, everyone in the New Mexican territory knew Lucien Maxwell.

He sold the grant one hundred twenty-nine years ago; and much of what lingers around his memory today is, unfortunately, linked to what happened after that time, the eviction of families and legal battles that continued until the end of the century. Though the patent for the land was issued in 1879, the United States Supreme Court did not render a decision until 1887, and other lawsuits lingered even after that.

In legend, he lived long past his time, the famous, or "infamous," Maxwell Land Grant carrying his name. The legend might have held more truth had the Mexican land grant not carried the name of the man who developed, purchased, and subsequently sold it — prior to its notoriety.

The legend might have grown in a different manner had the United States government followed New Mexico Superintendent of Indian Affairs A.B. Norton's advice in October 1866:

> I would recommend that the Maxwell Grant be purchased as a reservation upon which to permanently locate them [Indians]. This grant of land which has been confirmed by the government is about forty or sixty miles in extent, contains about one million six hundred thousand acres over three thousand of which are now under irrigation and situated on the Cimarron which never fails on which is built one of the best flouring mills in the territory built of stone . . . in the most permanent and substantial manner at a cost of $50,000. Also a good sawmill both run by the water power of the Cimarron, also good dwellings and storehouses[,] barns and corrals are located thereon, all of which can be purchased by the government for $250,000. The improvements cost over 1/2 that sum. I have examined the property thoroughly and consider it very cheap. These Indians will be satisfied to locate here and cultivate the soil. I know that after the first year they can and will support themselves. This grant is sufficiently large and has sufficient irrigable land for all the Utes and Apaches of this territory if it should be considered desirable to locate them thereon.

For whatever the reasons, the government chose to ignore the opportunity. Lucien Maxwell turned the sale over to speculators and walked away.

Essentially, Lucien Maxwell was a man, in the largest sense of the word. Though little is known of his personal life, the legends grew because of the man himself. From the man and from the legends came an American who represents unique years in American history.

Lucien Maxwell's life and the lands he came to own paralleled the Santa Fe Trail, forming a connection not only between east and west, but also between the youth and maturity of a new nation.

When his life began in Kaskaskia, Illinois, Illinois had only a few weeks earlier been approved by Congress as the twenty-first state of the union, and century-old Kaskaskia was named its capital. It was 1818 and millions of buffalo roamed western prairies. Within a few years, Becknell made his first expedition to Santa Fe; President James Monroe initiated a survey of the wagon route to New Mexico; and the United States government purchased easement rights from several Indian tribes who "owned" lands west of the Mississippi.

Shortly before Lucien's tenth birthday, founding fathers Thomas Jefferson and John Adams died. A new era was underway. Steamboats chugged up and down the Mississippi, New Orleans and Saint Louis reverberating with river traffic; and though most people didn't have any idea what railroads were, the first passenger train began operation.

By the time Lucien died, at age fifty-six, only five years after selling out, anarchy and murder dominated every community in northeastern New Mexico; the Maxwell Land Grant and Railway Corporation was in bankruptcy; and the Santa Fe Ring controlled the territory. Colorado was preparing to celebrate the bicentennial year by becoming the thirty-eighth state. The first six presidents of the twentieth century had already been born, a transcontinental railroad connected Atlantic and Pacific Oceans, gold seekers were pouring into South Dakota's Black Hills, and New York City had celebrated the construction of its first "high-rise" office building, a seven-story structure that housed the Equitable Life Assurance Society. Shortly after Lucien Maxwell's death, the railroad connected New Mexico with cities east and west, and the Santa Fe Trail was, like the vast buffalo herds that had been completely decimated, a relic of another time. The west, as it had been, died. Lucien Maxwell's lifetime framed the years when it had lived.

Lucien Maxwell was a trader, in the best implications of that term, satisfactorily serving a good purpose for both sides of a bargain. His handshake connected three cultures and, at the same time, linked the world as it was and the world as it was going to be. He sought greater rewards than chunks of gold, risking his life many times over to be the man he wanted to be, and he reaped unprecedented rewards for taking such risks.

It is the risk-taker who most reveals what America is about, whether he is an immigrant venturing across an ocean to reach an unknown land, an Indian utilizing bow and arrow to survive in a forest, or a twenty-first-century entrepreneur utilizing hard-earned dollars to start a new enterprise.

Lucien Maxwell was a risk-taker. He has been admired and maligned, both by those who shared his table and by those who lived long after him. In this book I have avoided the legendary, utilizing only what has been established as fact. I hope the reader will find in Lucien Maxwell's life the mysterious something that brings about admiration.

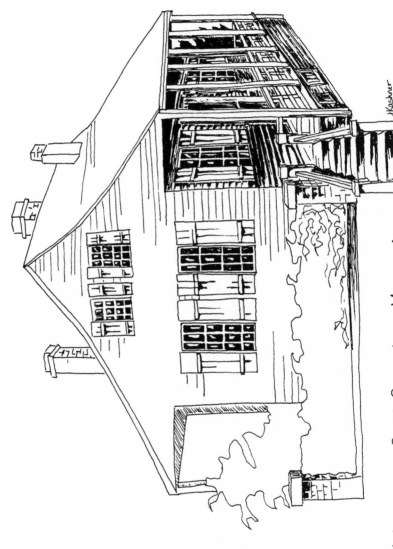

A house in Saint Genevieve, Missouri

1

THE VECTORS CONVERGE
1818 TO 1829

Forty years after revolution separated North American colonies from England, the United States of America was at the brink of claiming all lands as far west as the Pacific ocean, two thousand miles past the mighty river which drained the center of the North American continent. It had taken all of two hundred years for settlement to gain "the old west."

In another fifty years, during Lucien Maxwell's lifetime, telegraph and railroads traversed the continent into a "new west" that extended across prairies and mountains. In 1818, the year that he was born, Saint Louis, Missouri, was already the Gateway to that west. As steamboats advanced upstream on the "Father of Waters" and then farther up its major tributary, the Missouri, an overland trail connected Saint Louis to the southwest; and within two decades another wagon route beckoned thousands to the northwest Oregon country. Traffic and trade from river towns along the Mississippi funneled noisily into Saint Louis. And just fifty miles south of Saint Louis, two of those towns, one on each side of the Mississippi River, Kaskaskia, Illinois, and Sainte Genevieve, Missouri, witnessed the early years of a boy named Lucien Maxwell.

"From 1810 to 1820, Kaskaskia was the rendezvous of an immense floating population, which gave it the air of a bee-hive[*sic*]. Every emigrant to the [Illinois] Territory directed his course to it as the point from which to explore the country. . . . A census taken then showed the population to be seven thousand and some hundreds. . . . About 1820, other towns began to spring up and claim attention. The confusion, bustle and storm raised by the swarming emigrants in Kaskaskia began to die away, leaving the village to gradually and quietly resume its original character."[1]

This was the community in which Lucien received his ideas of what was good and what he wanted to achieve, his parents' families having arrived in Kaskaskia prior to its boom time and playing definitive roles in the town's development. From them, he heard stories of Illinois history, and with them he listened to conversations about its future. The youngster's multi-rooted family tree served him well when he later nurtured and built his own community in northern New Mexico. Lucien Maxwell, from the beginning, was surrounded by western traders and founders. Both his mother's and father's people moved into the territory as youngsters; there they established themselves, married, accumulated lands and wealth, built pylons of community in outposts of the young American nation. Lucien repeated the sequence during his own lifetime on yet another western frontier as did his brother and cousin, founders of Galveston, Texas, and one of his father's neighbors in Sainte Genevieve, Steven Austin, for whom the capital of Texas was named. A family tradition; a community tradition: they were not building empires; they were building America.

During Lucien's childhood a multiplicity of cultures blended into a broadly based knowledge, which provided a central thrust of his education. Lucien's relatives in Missouri came from Ireland, his great uncle a Catholic priest assigned to settlements on the Spanish side of the river. The Reverend James Maxwell was recipient, before the Louisiana Purchase, of Spanish land grants that involved disputes similar to those arising later in New Mexico.[2] A justice of the peace and president of the Missouri Territorial Council, he died before Lucien was born; but Lucien's father, Hugh Maxwell, nephew of the Reverend, grew up in Sainte Genevieve, a French settlement in then Spanish-owned Louisiana Territory, and went to work for Pierre Menard, subsequently marrying his employer's oldest daughter.

Hugh and Odile Maxwell raised a family, and new babies came as regularly as changing seasons. Married seven years, Odile was only twenty-five years old when their son Lucien was born, on September 14, 1818, fifth of twelve children. Also like siblings were uncles and aunts, children of his grandfather's second marriage and Lucien's contemporaries. Closeness of family, cousins, and grandchildren imprinted strongly on the boy.

Growing up in a home and among family where generosity and hospitality received great emphasis, he learned how to handle himself in a variety of situations and, most important, among a variety of people. Recognizing that Lucien repeated the saga of his forebears' lives reveals much about his attitudes and self expectations. Coming as vectors into a circle, parents, grandparents, uncles, and aunts gathered in that small community of the Illinois territory.

While most Kaskaskians, when Lucien was a child, were reading recently published journals of Lewis and Clark and Zebulon Pike, whose expeditions stretched far to the west into the "Shining Mountains," Lucien's grandfather Menard had firsthand information on the wilderness. He had spent a year in the upper reaches of the Missouri River as a partner in the Saint Louis Missouri Fur Company.[3]

The fur industry flourished throughout early years of Lucien's life and well into his teenage years. By trapping beaver and selling pelts to traders in Saint Louis, mountain men made their living. Buyers of pelts, in turn, marketed their goods to makers of stylish hats much in demand by ladies and gentlemen back east and in Europe. Trappers and hunters shared the hunting grounds of Indian tribes who, for the most part, were not threatened by the presence of men who learned to speak their language and in many instances married their women. "The early traders, having but seldom experienced any molestations from the Indians, generally crossed the plains in detached bands, each individual rarely carrying more than two or three hundred dollars' worth of stock."[4] Peaceful exchange continued as long as numbers of mountain men remained small and undisturbing.

In the days before Whites had encroached to any great extent, Indians and trappers set up a trading system based upon an implicit degree of trust. Trappers, arriving at a village, opened their packs to display the tools and trinkets they wanted to sell. Using sticks as tokens, they established a method of communication, and trading began. When an acceptable number of sticks were placed on a buffalo robe or beaver skin, the parties to the transaction indicated their agreement; then they placed their newly-purchased items on opposite sides of the lodge.[5] The day's purchases proved satisfactory to all.

Pierre Menard had "opened a lucrative trade with the Indians. Endowed with rare business talent, a well balanced judgment, and an honest purpose, he rose rapidly to a high degree of eminence and distinction . . ., and became the idol of the Indians. . . . No man ever enjoyed the confidence and esteem of the Indians more than he. They worshiped him; and though he controlled them as a father does his children, he never took advantage of that confidence and simplicity to wrong them."[6]

Because his father and grandfather traded with the Kaskaskia tribe, Lucien, as a young boy, learned about the Illini, a member of Algonquin-speaking peoples who hunted over the eastern half of North America and as far west as the Rocky Mountains. If he accompanied his father on trips to Saint Louis to buy merchandise for trading, and he probably did, Lucien learned for himself about trappers who came in for supplies, listening to what they said about the places they had been.

Mountain men returned to Saint Louis with stories of Mexico, land south of the United States, and adventurers soon began following westward-reaching trails. In Taos and Santa Fe, they joined descendants of early Spanish colonists and Indians who came to trade under temporary truce. Utes traded raw materials for axes, bridles, knives, and trinkets. Navajos traded woven blankets for Ute baskets. Everyone traded captives as slaves.[7] People who lived in northern Mexico traded silver for previously unavailable manufactured cloth and tools.

Facilitating this trade and occurring simultaneously with Lucien Maxwell's early years, the Santa Fe Trail opened for business. In the spring of 1821, when Lucien was three years old, William Becknell made his first official trip, seven hundred miles westward from the little town of Franklin, Missouri, to Santa Fe. When he returned that fall, saddle bags filled to the brim with Mexican silver, he immediately began making plans for the next year's wagon loads of goods. While, in 1819, the first steamship had crossed the Atlantic Ocean in twenty-six days, what became an annual crossing of "the great American desert" took twice that long. Traffic on the Santa Fe Trail lasted until shortly after Lucien Maxwell's death some fifty years later, remaining during that time the principal connection between the Mississippi River and New Mexico until the Atchison, Topeka, and Santa Fe Railroad traversed Raton Pass and descended southward toward Albuquerque.[8]

Because of such satisfactory exchange, Commissioner George Sibley, on behalf of the United States, was able to make a treaty with the Osage Indians. West of Franklin, in a small grove of oak trees later to be called Council Grove, "the Indians agreed to allow all citizens of the United States and Mexico to pass unmolested . . . [and received] a gratification of eight hundred dollars in merchandise."[9] Only later, as wagon trains increased in breadth and width and tonnage, did confrontations with Indians become more frequent. In the meantime, men who had already spent many years trapping and trading in western plains and mountains guided and taught less experienced travelers.

The city of Saint Louis drew them all together, a variety of men from a variety of backgrounds: Chouteaus and Menards, French-Canadian Catholic families of Saint Louis and Kaskaskia; Irish-Catholic Maxwells; Spaniard Manuel Lisa of Sainte Genevieve; and descendants of Mayflower Puritans, Charles and William Bent. Lucien Maxwell's grandparents and parents associated, in one way or another, with them all. A young boy in a small town, Lucien observed traveling dignitaries, as well as family and friends, at Pierre Menard's home. "The Menard doors were always open . . . and his hospitality and good works became almost legend."[10]

Lucien had to have become aware of his grandfather's respected position, not only in Kaskaskia, but in the entire state and even the nation. After all, two presidents appointed him to treat with Indian tribes. Histories of Kaskaskia published within fifteen years of Lucien's grandfather's death praised his contributions: "Long interested in Indian affairs, Menard spent much of his own time and money in giving aid to the distressed red men in his area . . . supporting the remnants of the Kaskaskia tribe out of his own pocket. . . . Always looking out for Indian welfare, Menard constantly complained to the government about the injustices perpetrated against the tribes. . . ."[11]

Selling provisions to fur traders and bartering with Indians, Menard built a business that encompassed much more than a store for Kaskaskia's residents. His extensive enterprises reached as far as Canada, New Orleans, Pittsburgh, and trading centers farther west, thus contributing to his town's central role in the Illinois Territory's commerce. As owner of lands whose acres numbered in the thousands, operator of

both ferry and mill, and controller of a monopolistic interest in the lo-
cally-based salt trade, he prospered.[12]

Menard's business ventures accompanied his interest, along with
that of other residents of the area, in making Illinois an official territory;
but, by the time Lucien was old enough to remember, his grandfather
had set aside any political ambitions. Menard, having remarried, had
seven young children by his second wife. Elected to the first Illinois
Legislative Council, he served as its president until Congress made Illinois the nation's twenty-first state. Pierre Menard, fifty-two years old,
was then elected first lieutenant governor of Illinois. After a year in which
he "presided over the state senate with common sense, dignity, and a
respect for the law all too rare on the frontier, [Lieutenant Governor
Menard] retired from elective public life thereafter to devote himself to
his large family . . ., his personal business, and the care of the hundreds
of Indians who looked to him as their advisor and protector."[13]

With father and grandfather closely associated in business and
both being heads of growing families, Lucien received a double-bar-
reled impression of what was useful, important, and worthwhile. About
Pierre Menard, contemporaries said, "From his commercial transactions
he realized a fortune, which he cheerfully shared with the needy. No
charitable call ever reached his ear without a ready response."[14] Many
years later and a thousand miles west of Kaskaskia, Illinois, almost identical words appeared in newspapers following Lucien's death in New
Mexico. The boy grown into a man made decisions based upon early
admiration of his grandfather. More than coincidental parallels exist
between them. Grandfather, and his grandson after him, sought to acquire land and build on and around that land a community. Though
grandson Lucien never entered politics, he became known and respected
throughout New Mexico, just as Menard had been in Illinois.

Lucien's father, Hugh Maxwell, also reinforced for his son their
family's emphasis upon trade. Hugh and his father-in-law Menard
shared similar business interests and both invested in a locally organized bank. Likewise, Lucien formed a permanent business relationship with his own father-in-law and, a quarter of a century later, founded
the First National Bank of Santa Fe. Traditions continued, grandfather
to grandson, father to son.

Ten-year-old Lucien absorbed everything that was going on

around him, unknowingly preparing for what lay ahead as he listened to neighbors, family, and friends. Then, much more so than now, every activity centered around family, and Lucien's actions as a mature individual reflected quite clearly this early influence. Ultimately he reached toward a horizon that merely extended westward from his childhood. Instead of the Mississippi's bustling activity, he chose an overland highway to Santa Fe. In trade dollars exchanged, the centuries-old Mexican city never approached Saint Louis dimensions, and the Cimarron River in comparison to the mighty Father of Waters was only a tiny stream. But, far to the west, shining mountains rose from flat, treeless prairies. There, converging vectors of his life merged into a larger horizon where French, Spanish, Irish, Mexican, and Indian traditions came together in a new way, in a land of enchantment called New Mexico.

Pierre Menard home, Kaskaskia, Illinois

2

ADOLESCENCE FOR LUCIEN
AND FOR AMERICA
1830 TO 1839

Something was different in the world and America epitomized what was happening. A great new optimism encouraged people to think about bettering themselves and their families. John Deere's steel plow and Cyrus McCormick's reaper freed farmers for other aspects of agricultural production; three-inch splinters of wood tipped with chemicals could be ignited, thus easing lengthy manipulations required to start fires; typewriters, sewing machines, and Colt revolvers demonstrated apparently unlimited potential. Individuals grasped the idea that personal wealth could mean more than money or gold; it could enable an individual to improve the way he lived. A good and comfortable life was suddenly within reach of the ordinary human being and anybody could be somebody even without social credentials.

Use of manufactured gas replaced candles, Baltimore leading the way to its large-scale usage in lighting city streets at night. Baseburner stoves permitted regulated heat from small amounts of coal, eliminating the toilsome chore of cooking over open fires. Even middle-class homes could have iceboxes that meant longer food storage. New machine-run tools produced chairs that sold for as little as thirty to seventy-five cents each. Families could comfortably sit around a table instead of leaning forward from backless benches. Carpets covered floors in one fourth of American homes, and bricks provided a safer, longer-lasting alternative to wood. A new sense of privacy pervaded such places as Boston's Tremont House Hotel, where guests had access to eight bathrooms in addition to eight water closets.[1]

Labor-saving devices of all kinds increased productivity, which, in turn, meant availability of surplus goods and produce. Exchange of that surplus opened markets where people connected with each other. In Illinois, canals and roads were the topic of conversation. Everything happening there by the Mississippi in the "old west" became part of the young man who was destined for importance in formation of the "new west." Menards and Maxwells gave community their full attention, attitudes toward responsibility and productivity resounding throughout their town's populace. Lucien saw what his grandfather, his father, and his uncle before him had helped accomplish. From them he learned his measure of success: to own land, to make that land produce, to trade.

The nation, too, was learning its lessons. Having withstood its first military trial in the War of 1812, the United States faced what was to be a lengthy and difficult passage through its formative years. Early leadership fell to President Andrew Jackson, tough old soldier from Tennessee, who met head-on the challenge of an enlarging population and government.

Changes moved like winds across North America, forcing former residents to move in their wake. By the thirties all Indian tribes had been ordered out of Illinois and "migrating Yankees advanced into the state. The earliest wave of settlers loved the wilderness and thought of it as a sanctuary. They more or less disappeared into it and became part of it. . . . But the Yankees were in a big hurry to conquer the wilderness and build profitable farms and cities. . . . By the 1830s, milled lumber, machine-made nails, windows, and hardware were much easier to obtain, and the Yankees had the money to buy them."[2]

Merchants seeking to connect with distant markets sought better transportation. The state government issued bonds for a canal to connect Lake Michigan with the Illinois River, which in turn flowed into the Mississippi, creating a waterway to the Gulf of Mexico; and it subsidized railroads running south to north as well as east to west. Buildings rose in Chicago and construction of the capitol at Springfield began. The state of Illinois was changing rapidly; new people came steadily.

"Traveling overland to central and northern Illinois, shady woodlands must have seemed endless. In many places the canopy of trees was so thick that it was like traveling all day in twilight. Then suddenly, they were confronted with a sight unlike any they had ever seen: the country opened out into a vast, sun-filled grassland. They had reached the eastern edge of the great prairies that were later found to extend all the way to the Rocky Mountains. . . . The graceful grasses and flowers that grew to be six or more feet high often had more of the plant underground than above! Roots as big around as a man's finger extended twelve or fifteen feet down into the soil."[3]

An 1839 visitor described Kaskaskia, the town of Lucien Maxwell's teenage years:

> *Though past its political and commercial glory, [it] was still a considerable town, and, socially, very lively. . . . The town had no factory of any description, or other local industry to employ its people, as the community was agricultural and pastoral, deriving its support chiefly from its "commons," a magnificent tract of adjoining land, several thousands of acres in extent, level as a floor, and not surpassed in fertility by the famed valley of the Nile. . . . The dwellings, with few exceptions, were of the ancient French pattern, made of wood, one story and attic, many with dormer windows in the roof, and all surrounded with porches, . . . Homemade carts constructed altogether of wood, drawn by one horse, or pony, were in general use. . . . A few, very few of the most opulent citizens had eastern-made, or imported carriages. . . . The two-horse farm wagons that came to Edgar's mill, and into the town, with grain or other produce, invariably belonged to American settlers, and were an innovation that the French were very slow to adopt. The natives were very partial to horseback riding. . . .*[4]

Native-born Whites represented a majority, most of French descent and some of mixed French and Indian heritage, all belonging to the town's Catholic parish to which their parents and grandparents had belonged before them. The few English-speaking newcomers became a definite minority, their number smaller even than the fifty to seventy-five Negro slaves. Among a population of some six hundred, the lately-arriving Americans, as they were called, had to learn the native-spoken Canadian *patois* together with a new way of life.[5]

Lucien's grandparents and parents occupied a prominent position in Kaskaskian society, his grandmother's people, the Chouteaus, among the first families of Saint Louis. Menard's assistance to the Sisters of Visitation in establishing their school for girls resulted in that institution's bearing his name which was well-known by all. The stores that Pierre Menard and Lucien's father ran provided substantial income, and the family was often called upon to entertain visiting dignitaries.

Lucien probably preferred skipping rocks across the river from a vantage point on its edge to dressing up for family social affairs. Perhaps he played with other boys among the crumbling gravestones in the cemetery atop the hill. Surely he touched with boyish curiosity the deep, green, velvety moss that covered the roof of the moldering old church built in the previous century, and he must have delighted in catching fish at Edgar's Mill. Joining Kaskaskia's youngsters at a vacant lot near the center of town, Lucien may have been told by his grandfather that its sandy, weedless surface covered rubble left from the old fort abandoned by the British during America's Revolutionary War.[6]

Crossing the Kaskaskia River by flatboat ferry or taking the land route on horseback, Lucien could easily make the short trip to his grandfather's house. Or, he could jaunt three miles west to the bank of the Mississippi. From there, the old village of Sainte Genevieve was visible on the river's western side, nine miles upstream. Family and friends were never far away and Pierre Menard's mansion welcomed them all. A gentleman who attended a reception and ball, in the latter years of the decade, observed that seventy-year-old Colonel Menard seemed "weak and careworn, perhaps from ill-health [sic]; but was mentally bright, and very talkative. Mrs. Menard, who was with him, was his second wife, and apparently several years his junior in age. She was yet a handsome woman, with tall, shapely figure, black eyes and black hair, dark complexioned, and animated in speech and manners."[7]

Together with his brothers and sisters, and uncles and aunts also in their teens, Lucien observed a variety of social affairs, special evenings when candlelight reflected off highly polished floors, and gaily-dressed musicians played for enthusiastic dancers. A guest at one such affair described Miss Adeline Maxwell as "the reigning belle of Kaskaskia."[8]

Another of Lucien's sisters married their cousin Michel Branamour Menard, who first came to Kaskaskia from Canada as an eighteen-year-old. Family relationships being as close as they were, Lucien must have known about his cousin's employment, representing Pierre Menard as trader with Shawnees and Delaware Indians. Stories about kinfolk circulated in Kaskaskia. Supposedly cousin Michel almost accomplished a union of the northwestern tribes into one nation; but it was known for certain that he lived with the Shawnees, was adopted by them, and served as their elected chief. By the time Lucien turned fifteen, his cousin had established a trading post and was initiating claim to land for the town which ultimately came to be Galveston, Texas. A few years later, Michel signed the republic's Declaration of Independence and helped draft its constitution.[9]

While Texas was approaching its independence, Lucien was becoming a man. In September 1833, less than two weeks before his fifteenth birthday, Lucien, abruptly and without celebration, left childhood behind. Cholera, with painful and debilitating dehydration, claimed his forty-three-year-old father. Even in peaceful Kaskaskia a child had to face losses of those he loved. Months before, a little brother had died, less than a year old, and a younger sister, not yet a teenager. His father's untimely death must have devastated the family, but that loss was not enough. Early in November his older sister Mary T. Lucretia died as well.

Three nights after his sister's death, just days before Lucien left for school, a meteor shower occurred, one of the most brilliant in American history. In Independence, frightened Missourians saw it as heavenly retribution against their mob attacks and floggings of the Mormons. In Santa Fe, horrified Mexicans felt themselves cursed because of the state's refusal to recognize the Church's special privileges. Out on the plains where Bent's Fort rose near completion on the Santa Fe Trail, Cheyenne Indians foresaw their own end and sang of death as was befitting great warriors.[10] Shooting stars marked in Lucien's memory one of the most difficult times of his life.

Whether the boy's departure for school was decided upon before or after his father's death remains undetermined, as does the payer of his tuition. Older brother Ferdinand remained in Kaskaskia, managing their father's store.[11] Their mother, then forty years old, was left with five other young children.

Lucien enrolled at the Vincentian school, Saint Mary's of the

Barrens, where young men studying to be priests taught boys who were there for more general education. Situated eighty miles south of Saint Louis and across the river from Kaskaskia, the first Vincentian college in the United States attracted, in 1830, over one hundred thirty students, some from as far away as Cuba. Families from Louisiana and other southern states sent their sons for education.[12] Some years later, Carlos Beaubien, Maxwell's father-in-law, sent both his sons to Saint Mary's. The school emphasized Saint Vincent's teachings of duty and responsibility to help the poor, particularly the rural poor who had no daily access to the church, a duty which Lucien's grandfather, and later Lucien himself, took quite seriously.

A fellow student later wrote in his autobiography, "The discipline was not very rigid; we were allowed to smoke at any and all times." Boys learned, he said, "much of nature and kindly companionship combined with a certain manliness," traits which proved of inestimable help during Lucien's entire life. There was more to school life, however, than the subjects that appeared on his record, Catholic studies, Latin, English, spelling, arithmetic, and geography. Friendly instructors led outings to nearby caves where older students sometimes captured bats, which they later released, quite intentionally, to frighten the younger dormitory residents.[13]

School records indicate that Lucien attended for only two years, from late November through mid-July, until he was almost seventeen years old. After Saint Vincent's Feast Day on July 19, 1835, the boy did not return to school and his exact whereabouts following departure from school remain unknown. Prepared to make his own way in the world, one option for Lucien at that time was to remain in Kaskaskia and become a merchant. Kaskaskia, however, was no longer a booming center of travel and offered little excitement for a young man who had seen not only his grandfather's and his father's achievements, but also those of uncles on both sides of his family.

Trails westward called. Since Lucien's grandfather Menard had held a prominent position during his younger days in the fur trade, at the least Menard must have maintained connections with Chouteau and Pratte, former partners in the original Missouri Fur Company, men who had recently bought the western division of Astor's American Fur Company. The seventeen-year-old Kaskaskian probably had little trouble finding work. With much to learn, he had easy access to teachers who were as close as river boats on the Mississippi.

At one time or another, Saint Louis welcomed most of them, men who were Lucien's role models and instructors. William Sublette, then about thirty-five years old, was ready to settle down after almost twenty years in the fur trade. He and his partner had already built Fort Laramie in southeastern Wyoming, and carpenters were finishing his new home north of Saint Louis. Living in modern style, yet without undue display of wealth, Sublette managed both his Main Street store and his outlying farm. Lucien could well have known this man who played a major role in Saint Louis banking, established two insurance companies, and dreamed of "an agrarian commonwealth."[14]

He definitely knew William and Charles Bent and Ceran St. Vrain, men whose new fort on the Arkansas River provided a welcome rest stop along the Santa Fe Trail and a principal trading post for trappers and Indians. Before construction of Bent's Fort, traders left in caravans, their oxen-drawn wagons departing in early spring on their annual trek across the plains, not to see another human habitation for several weeks. Hauling thousands of pounds of trade goods, they returned each fall with buffalo robes and Mexican silver.

At Bent's Fort, young Lucien worked with the man who was to be his lifelong friend. Kit Carson, nine years older than Lucien, was not yet famous, but already a widower and father of two children by his Indian wife. Kit had learned the fur trade from the most skillful of mountain men and had attended a few of their annual rendezvous.

At rendezvous, once a year, trappers and traders gathered, hundreds of men, to sell their previous winter's catch, to buy supplies for the coming winter's travel, and to have fun. Whites and Indians, men, women, and children, lived together at rendezvous for a week or more in mid-summer, then departed for their respective winter camps and their work of trapping beaver. They "lived continuously in the mountains, all of them near-savages more at home amidst the silent forests or in Indian villages than in the haunts of their fellow men."[15] Operating in what was the last of the wild west before miners and settlers and ranchers grasped the significance of seemingly limitless, treeless prairie, they lived on what nature provided.

A trapper's camp afforded only minimal protection from storms, his only shelter sometimes being a few deerskins stretched over a willow frame; but it did provide a place where he could have all his essentials within easy reach and his horses hobbled nearby. Animal skins kept powder and bullets dry, and meat hung on a wooden pole carefully suspended between the crotched tops of two other poles, high enough to discourage hungry wolves or coyotes.[16]

Each mountain man carried a "possible sack" and everything essential for his survival: steel beaver traps and chains to anchor them; two thick blankets; a belt; a sheathed knife particularly sharpened for skinning; a well-made rifle along with the necessary cleaning worm and wiping stick made of solid hickory; a bullet pouch, lead, and the mold required to make new bullets; powder and powder horn; a hooded capote made from a large blanket; a comb; a tin cup; an awl; flint and steel; tobacco pouch and pipe; a hatchet; spurs and a saddle.[17]

During the last of his teenage years, Lucien lived with the fur trade's mountain men, familiarizing himself with trails between Saint Louis and Fort St. Vrain on the South Platte River, and between Taos and Bent's Fort on the Arkansas River. Men of the new west met at Bent's Fort, men who would be a part of Lucien's new life. As competition heightened between the two major fur companies, they finally agreed to divide up western trade: Bents and St. Vrain operating south of the North Platte and Chouteau's American Fur Company to the north. William and Charles Bent, along with Ceran St. Vrain, established a trade that connected New Mexico and Saint Louis; and William Bent, known as "Little White Man" to the Cheyennes, also dealt with Arapahos, Utes, Northern Apaches, Kiowas, and Comanches.

Commerce continued to open new routes, advancing the inland frontier toward Oregon as well as Mexico. Travel increased over the series of ruts that widened to avoid mud during spring rains; and, as steamboats gained access of the Missouri River, a new town developed as a more western point of departure at Independence, Missouri. There, one hundred fifty miles up the Missouri River from Saint Louis and only twelve miles from the Indian border, the actual trail to Santa Fe began. From Independence to Santa Fe, its traffic and trade broke down barriers. Traders, trappers, Americans, and New Mexicans learned about each other and about the territory that lay between Mexican and United States boundaries. New communities housed people who had never before lived together. Las Vegas, New Mexico, grew into another rest stop for Santa Fe Trail travelers between Bent's Fort and Santa Fe.

As cities of the old west grew, civilization included Cincinnati, Chicago, Saint Louis, Memphis, and New Orleans among its ranks, and youngsters who had heard their parents' stories of moving west and starting out on their own followed the dream. They had grown up utilizing skills their parents had struggled to acquire; now they, too, headed west, beyond the Mississippi River, beyond family and comforts of wherever they came from.

Lands left by departing Indians opened to profiteers and railroads, and, by the time Lucien was twenty-one, reckless speculation had dumped the country into financial depression. Unregulated banks failed, not having kept enough gold in reserve to back up notes issued to depositors; individual accounts vanished as banks closed their doors; farmers watched prices of grain and meat fall; storekeepers without funds could no longer stock their shelves. The state of Illinois seemed to be on the verge of defaulting on its bond payments.[18] In direct contrast to its beginning, the decade's finale pointed in another direction.

Rapid transition surrounded river towns where Lucien had grown up. Beaver hats lost their charm for easterners who now wanted only fashionable silk. Markets diminished, leaving trappers to make their way as guides and freighters of merchandise. Peaceful, lovely, undisturbed Kaskaskia and schooldays spent with priests learning about how to treat his fellow human beings slowly succumbed to an onslaught of newness; everything old and stable abruptly changed.

The American Fur Company held its last rendezvous, with fewer than one hundred white trappers attending. Decreasing numbers of beaver and increasing numbers of people brought the day of the mountain man to an end, his chosen livelihood and isolated winter life no longer possible.[19]

"Grabbers" came to take and move on, men unconcerned about leaving something for the next generation. As Indians were pushed farther and farther west, out of the way of those who wanted their land, and onto lands claimed by Indians already occupying the territory, tribes that had shared prairies and mountains with only buffalo were meeting their new neighbors.

The Cherokees, who had supposedly learned the white man's

ways, developing accoutrements of civilization such as an alphabet and subsequent reading and writing skills, recorded their history and made laws. Many became Christians. Such so-called progress made little difference. The United States government resorted to coercion, pushing thirteen thousand Cherokees along the "Trail of Tears" to their new home in what is now northeastern Oklahoma. Four thousand died along the way, before ever reaching the seven million acres on the other side of the Mississippi River.[20]

As the decade ended, Halley's comet appeared, not to be seen again for half a century. Old leaders stepped aside and the last surviving signer of the Declaration of Independence died. International changes also reflected new attitudes. In Spain the Inquisition finally came to an end; in France monarchs no longer ruled by divine right; and, with coronation of a new queen, England ushered in the Victorian Age.

Seventy-two-year-old Pierre Menard sat for his portrait in Saint Louis. He had seen the west for himself, withstood eighteen months in the wilderness, in what is now North Dakota and Montana. Grandfather shared critical time with his grandson before Lucien left Kaskaskia. Pierre Menard couldn't know what his grandson's future held, but he surely discerned in the mirror of Lucien's eyes that another link was about to be forged in America's westward movement.

The last item on Lucien's account from Saint Mary's of the Barrens was a map costing one dollar, only cents less than a pair of shoes purchased a month earlier,[21] shoes that would wear out long before that map's imprint faded from his memory.

3

COMING OF AGE
1840 TO 1849

Bent's Fort . . . the outside exactly fills my idea of an ancient castle. It is built of adobes, unburnt brick, and Mexican style so far. The walls are very high and very thick with rounding corners. There is but one entrance, this is to the East rather. . . .

Inside is a large space some ninety or an hundred feet "square" all around this and next the wall are rooms, some twenty-five in number. . . .

Susan Magoffin, eighteen years old,
en route on the Santa Fe Trail
July 27, 1846[1]

There, at Bent's Fort, in what is now southeastern Colorado, Lucien Maxwell worked where Indians and traders gathered. In the vast spaces that lay between the Mississippi River and the Pacific Ocean, there was nothing else like the huge structure built by the brothers Bent and their partner Ceran St. Vrain. Its thirty-inch-thick walls rose fourteen feet above the Arkansas River; and even taller towers, themselves seventeen feet in diameter, stood defensively alert at northeastern and southwestern corners. A trapezoid-shaped grouping of rooms and walls enclosed an inner courtyard one hundred thirty-seven feet by one hundred seventy-eight feet.

Ceran St. Vrain and William Bent brought men from Taos to erect the carefully planned fort, its immensity awesome, particularly to travelers who had departed from more civilized environs several weeks earlier. Some twenty-five apartments varied in size from fifteen by twenty feet to larger residential type dwellings. A covered, wooden porch extended in front of the apartments, overlooking the inner courtyard, and a second story of additional rooms formed a roof over the tunnel-like entrance way. A sturdy outer gate built with planks sheathed in iron permitted passage of nine-feet-wide by seven-feet-high freight wagons that could load and unload merchandise without ever entering the inner courtyard.[2]

Mexicans from Taos, Indians, and Bent's traders all utilized the fort's amenities. Several weeks away from either Santa Fe or Saint Louis, forts provided central bases to and from which the itinerant merchants traveled, in groups of twos and threes, along with their pack animals and goods. Exposed to winter storms and hungry predators, traders and trappers lived with minimal comforts between stayovers at Indian villages, where blankets and cloth, knives and axes paid for buffalo skins. Bent's Fort offered a home, a source of food for horses and mules, a place to share coffee and conversation.

Trading post business demanded intelligence and physical strength, livestock and agricultural operations requiring as much attention as financial management of trade goods. Men who knew that business made history, and the brown-haired, blue-eyed youngster made a place for himself in that history. Seasoned by forest and prairie and his experience in the Indian trade, Lucien grew proficient in skills required for survival in the new territory. But he did more than survive. Somewhere along the rough trails that he followed across perilous mountain passes, he acquired whatever it is that makes an individual a leader. He learned how to determine whom he could rely upon, and, most of all, he learned to rely upon himself.

At first, the decade of the forties held potential for a new and different relationship between American Indians and their expanding neighbor, a potential which sadly was never to be realized. "After the passing of the violent brigade and rendezvous fur trade and before the coming of the settlers and soldiers, [white trappers] lived well in the truly Wild West, came to know and savor it in ways that had been impossible before and would never be possible again."[3] Men like William Bent became part of the country they lived in and called it home. Such men guided Lucien Maxwell as he learned the ways of the west, gaining friendships which lasted throughout his life, with both Indians and Whites.

As diverse threads wove their way into the ever-enlarging tapestry that was the United States of America, the new nation struggled toward its maturity. Coast to coast interests expanded across the continent in shotgun style while Lucien Maxwell's vision narrowed into a sharp focus upon New Mexico. Gradually this Illinois boy became New Mexican, merging all of his youthful inheritance with a new and different culture.

Like the Santa Fe Trail, which connected traders on both sides of the great American desert, the young man forged a link between past and present. Eastward stretched his past, Kaskaskia, Menards, and Maxwells; and westward, his future, New Mexico and Taos, where Carlos Beaubien lived, the man with whom Lucien shaped his tomorrows.

At the Santa Fe Trail's western end, Don Carlos was to play a significant role in Lucien Maxwell's life, both as business associate and father-in-law. Beaubien, having left Canada where he had been ordained as a priest and where his family owned substantial amounts of land, lived for a time in Saint Louis and was employed as Auguste Chouteau's clerk. Starting out as a relatively poor man, Beaubien traveled to Taos where he opened a store and became "one of the first French-Canadian fur traders to settle in New Mexico following Mexican Independence from Spain." Marrying sixteen-year-old Pabla Lobato and accomplishing naturalized citizenship by the time he was thirty, Beaubien eventually acquired considerable wealth.[4]

His background in the same French-Canadian province where Lucien's grandfather Menard had lived prior to Kaskaskia, his French Catholicism, and his own loss of a parent at an early age contributed to a growing friendship between Carlos and Lucien. Their connection cemented firmly when the young man from Kaskaskia, in March 1842, married Beaubien's oldest daughter, Luz, then in her early teens and later described as a beautiful woman with hazel eyes and dark hair.[5]

Marriage did not keep him in one place very long. Accompanying his friend Kit Carson on a trip to Saint Louis, twenty-three-year-old Lucien left Taos a short time after his wedding, supposedly for a visit to Kaskaskia, and possibly a last visit with his grandfather who died only two summers later.[6] Lucien and Carson did not return home until October because both were hired by the west's new "Pathfinder," John Frémont. Frémont, only a few years older than Lucien, had himself only recently married Jessie Benton, daughter of Senator Thomas Hart Benton, America's most outspoken expansionist.

On Frémont's first expedition, twenty-eight men traveled across the plains to Fort St. Vrain and onward to South Pass, which opened across the continental divide in Wyoming and established the gateway for travelers on the famous Oregon Trail. Frémont's maps and his journals that were published in 1845 established Kit Carson's fame. Though Frémont had nothing bad or critical to say about Lucien, the youngster did not receive the Pathfinder's high praises that were to make his friend Kit a symbol of western heroism.

But Lucien earned his pay. Early in the expedition, at the mouth of the Kansas River, Frémont insisted on trying a new rubber raft that he loaded heavily with what otherwise would have been packed on their animals' backs. When the raft capsized, his men had to dive for critical supplies. Lucien and Carson, with their strenuous and exhausting efforts, both became ill from exposure.[7] Frémont's reports of their journey implied satisfaction with the youngster's abilities, his brief words confirming Lucien Maxwell's experience and knowledge of Indians, their customs, and languages.

One episode, which Frémont reported in depth, indicated Lucien knew and was known by the Arapahos. When three hundred or so warriors rode in to attack the small reconnaissance party that included Frémont, Lucien and a few other horsemen, Lucien prepared to fire but stopped suddenly to yell out, "You're a fool, don't you know me?" He recognized a friend from previous years' trading and spoke the appropriate language. When the friend responded, also in recognition of their past acquaintance, attitudes changed. Attackers and targets shared buffalo meat for dinner.[8] As hunter and fellow explorer, Lucien proved his worth throughout the expedition, and he again joined the Pathfinder two years later on an even lengthier journey.

A few months after returning from their first summer with Frémont, Lucien's friend Kit Carson, then age thirty-three, also married. Josepha Jaramillo, daughter of an aristocratic Spanish family, was, like Lucien's wife, in her early teens. Mexican customs at that time encouraged such youthful matrimony, and five years passed before either Luz or Josepha had her first child.

Those five years proved critical, not only for Carson, Maxwell, Beaubien, and Frémont, but also for the United States, particularly lands west of the Mississippi. Competition between northern and southern states boiled. Eastern manufacturing interests demanded protective tariffs; southern plantation owners sought guarantees of continuing slave status for their owned black people; westerners wanted the Indians out of the way so they could settle on open, unowned lands. As the decade passed, so did the west as it was and as it might have been, with all of its potential for peaceful alliances.

Mountain men's last rendezvous signaled new directions and a new attitude toward American Indians. Traders who depended upon their reputation felt an obligation to fairness, and Lucien Maxwell, for as long as he was able, carried on their tradition. Americans in rapidly increasing numbers poured across the plains, spreading wider distances from established routes, disbursing buffalo herds and all the other indigenous creatures. Hunters, no longer able to rely upon familiar and established routes for locating readily available game, had to range farther and farther in pursuit of the animals on which they depended for survival. New people who came west "regarded the natives as obstacles and problems, often as varmints, who, like wolves and snakes, had to be controlled or eliminated."[9] In forming the connection with the future and new generations, Lucien represented the end of the old traders as well as the end of the Indians' life as it had related to those traders.

The Santa Fe Trail stands as a marker through that time period and through the lands which were Indian territory and uninhabitable according to most Americans. While waterways and railroads connected cities east of the Mississippi, trade between Saint Louis and Santa Fe continued to utilize mules or oxen to pull cumbersome wagons. At the same time, annexation of Texas and widely-opening trails to Oregon hurried American expansion.

Unending, supposedly unoccupied land fascinated Americans. They read with wonder about "optical illusions occasioned by the rarified and transparent atmosphere of the elevated plains."[10] South and west of the Republic of Texas, at the other end of what was called a desert, a truly old culture had been there when Pilgrims arrived on the

Atlantic coast. In a territory of about two hundred thousand square miles, most of New Mexico's 1841 population of seventy thousand, including ten thousand Pueblo Indians, lived within one hundred miles north and south of Santa Fe. No part of the country equalled either the beauty or the agricultural productivity of El Valle de Taos, situated a full two-day horseback ride north of the capital.[11]

Peasants using only primitive tools produced corn that comprised the central ingredient of one of their principal foods. Softening corn in boiling water with a little lime, New Mexicans ground it into a paste, which was then pressed into a thin cake and cooked for less than three minutes on a small sheet of iron or copper. The flat, round cakes known as *tortillas* served as spoons, eliminating need for knives and forks.[12]

Also serving purposes more utilitarian than decorative, unimposing adobe exteriors of Santa Fe and Taos homes did not reveal their comfortable interiors. Outer walls enclosed two separate sections, each of which opened onto a gardened patio area, and a single entrance permitted a wagon or coach to enter from the street. The rear grouping of rooms contained areas for food preparation and storage while the other contained living quarters. Rooms used mostly in winter, instead of opening to the patio, had doors to a hall, thus adding to insulation provided by thick adobe walls, making the house comfortably warm during cold weather and pleasantly cool in hot summer months. Few pieces of furniture decorated bare rooms, and sleepers unrolled blankets for a bed upon the whitewashed clay mortar that served as flooring.[13] Life couldn't have differed more from what Americans were accustomed to enjoying.

Lucien Maxwell, however, took to such new surroundings and New Mexico welcomed him. By the time he turned thirty, the youngster had seen and been part of both upper and lower economic levels of New Mexican society. As trader and traveler, he knew the difficulties of mountain living, but in Taos he dined with the Beaubiens. One of several successful so-called mixed families and observant of most French cultural amenities, they lived in a "luxurious home of thirty-eight rooms on the west side of Taos. . . . Pabla, clothed in fashionable dresses from Paris and New York, presided over the dining room which seated one hundred people. The Beaubiens furnished their home with fine furniture and other accessories — living well beyond the means of most New Mexicans."[14]

By being one of the first outsiders to remain and survive the many obstacles that were thrown in his path, Beaubien led the way toward establishment of a government that could make life more stable for the ordinary person. His persistence in remaining and building in northern New Mexico influenced others to remain.[15]

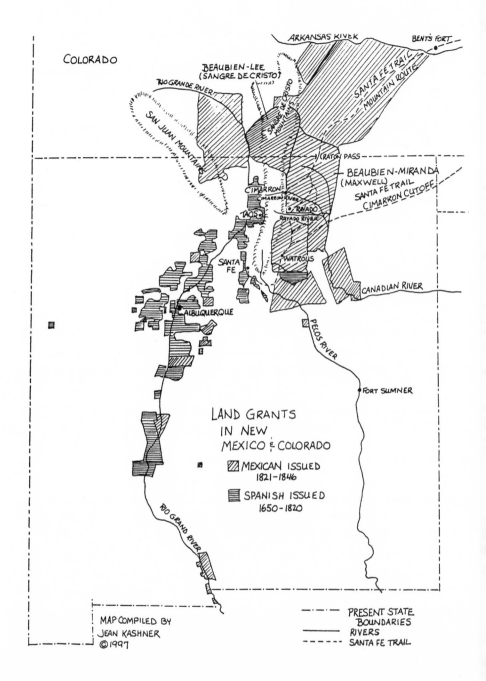

Mexican Land Grants in New Mexico and Colorado.

Carlos Beaubien, along with several other naturalized Mexican citizens, demonstrated unusual farsightedness. Both increasing traffic from the United States and claims by Texas on all lands as far west as the Rio Grande caused abrupt changes in Mexican land grant policy. Originally the King of Spain had awarded lands to "enterprising citizen-soldiers who would settle these lands with companions and create a buffer against the marauding of nomadic Indian tribes."[16] After Mexican independence from Spain, a sudden need to protect northern and eastern boundaries resulted in grants around the perimeter. Community grants provided common lands to be shared by settlers, while individuals received private grants with the understanding that they would proceed with agricultural settlement on their acreage.[17]

Carlos Beaubien joined Provincial Secretary of State Guadalupe Miranda in a petition for land situated east of the Sangre de Cristos. Though Governor Manuel Armijo promptly approved their grant, actual legal possession was delayed until after the Texans' invasion of northern New Mexico could be repelled. In February 1843, less than one year after Luz and Lucien's marriage, records indicate that Taos Justice of the Peace Cornelio Vigil traveled with the owners and five witnesses to mark the grant's seven corners with stone mounds and bestow formal possession in the traditional manner.[18]

Beaubien and Miranda's land covered a portion of northeastern New Mexican territory where, together with several other grants, it formed a bulwark of protection. Maps reveal that routes traveled by early trappers defined perimeters, with the Old Taos Trail marking the Beaubien and Miranda Grant's western boundary. Historian Victor Westphall explains, "The trail was already old when, in 1821, William Becknell first crossed Raton Pass and traveled southward along a path through the heartland of the area several miles west of the ultimate eastern boundary of the grant . . . A primitive trace from the Raton Pass branch of the Santa Fe Trail to Taos through a gap which George C. Sibley discovered while surveying that trail in 1825 . . . approximated the southern boundary. . . ."[19]

Beaubien, in addition to the first area, requested and obtained a second grant in the name of his sixteen-year-old son Narciso and a partner, Stephen Louis Lee, Taos trader and brother-in-law. The Beaubien and Miranda and Sangre de Cristo Grants, one almost two million acres and the other just under a million acres, included a considerable amount of land. Ultimately the United States patented over eleven million acres to such grant holders in what is now New Mexico and southern Colorado, many of which were owned by naturalized citizens in partnership with native Mexicans. "Private grants were frequently large in order to induce the more forceful individuals to settle new frontiers. Also, the arid climate necessitated more acres per head of cattle for grazing and other purposes."[20]

Obtaining and keeping land grants required settlement. Several brief attempts to farm and settle land on Beaubien's grant did not last. Anti-foreigner feeling pervaded native New Mexican culture, specifically led by Catholic priest José Antonio Martínez, who felt strongly that New Mexican land belonged to its people. Due to his influence and determination, government officials rescinded Beaubien and Miranda's grant but then, in a matter of months, restored it to intended grantees. Bitter words fueled the fight and bad feelings lingered long after all original parties were dead.

Even after restoration of the grant and sporadic attempts at settlement were made, the time for permanent, year-round residence had not arrived. First, Mexico and the United States had to resolve their differences, the two countries fighting a war before the United States added a million formerly Mexican acres to its territories. Second, following that war, New Mexicans rose in rebellion against the newly empowered American government of their lands. And, finally, something had to be done about the other people, Indians whose rights under the Mexican Colonization Law of 1828 were never fully enforced. That law authorized Mexican governors to assign lands to citizens; but the Indians who already occupied those lands were to remain as long as they liked, title not to be issued to the new grantees until such residency was voluntarily abandoned.[21]

Mexicans, Indians, and Americans, in spite of their conflicts, managed to live for several years according to their own traditions, but crosscurrents intersecting the twenty-year-old Santa Fe Trail anticipated future events and also reflected what was going on in the rest of North America. First, citizens of the new Republic of Texas attacked, claiming lands north and west as far as the Rio Grande. New Mexicans managed to repel and capture Texan invaders, but they never erased suspicions against naturalized citizens. Then, along the trail, outlaws attacked and murdered Don Antonio Chavez, son of a prominent New Mexican family, after which Santa Fe Trail trade was suspended for several months. The eight hundred-mile journey between Independence, Missouri, and Santa Fe resumed; but further Texas hostilities caused many traders like Beaubien to leave their homes and stores, fleeing at least temporarily for their lives.

Where the Santa Fe Trail had before provided an exchange between satisfied parties, a different mentality soon permeated its trade. Newly elected as tenth president of the United States, James K. Polk believed in "Manifest Destiny," which supposedly conferred upon Americans the divine right to occupy western lands, regardless of how such expansion affected the people who had occupied them for centuries.[22]

Midway through the decade, while Maxwell and Carson joined Frémont's third expedition which ventured into California, the United States went to war with Mexico on three different fronts. General Zachary Taylor landed with United States troops at Corpus Christi, Texas; Commodores John Sloat and then Robert Stockton claimed California; and General Stephen Kearny led his army south through New Mexico.

The Santa Fe Trail, built to connect two nations in friendly trade, became a conqueror's path. Seventeen hundred men in the Army of the West, along with hundreds of wagons and accompanying livestock, traveled over eight hundred miles from Missouri to Santa Fe in less than two months. Pausing with his troops at Bent's Fort before the perilous ascent of Raton Pass, General Kearny proclaimed his intentions to claim New Mexico for the United States of America. Then, on August 15, 1846, from a rooftop in the village of Las Vegas, he announced United States sovereignty and assured New Mexicans that their property, as well as their religion, was safe from interference. Brigadier General Kearny made quick work of conquering Santa Fe, initiating construction of Fort Marcy, sending his subordinates on a campaign against the Navajo Indians, and appointing Charles Bent as provisional governor. Thirty-eight days after entering New Mexico's capital, the general marched on to California.[23]

On the way, he and his troops met sixteen soldiers, Lucien Maxwell among them, and Kit Carson, in charge as personal courier from Frémont to the Secretary of the Navy and the President. Carson reported to Kearny, before the actual accomplishment, that Stockton and Frémont had conquered California. When Kearny ordered Carson to return with him to California, Lucien discouraged his friend from leaving during the night, an act which would have resulted in serious punishment for the famous scout.[24]

Carson and Maxwell had been traveling with Frémont for the past year and a half on an expedition that was supposedly a further exploration of the west but had actually skirted the edges of war with Mexico. In May 1846, when Congress declared a state of war with Mexico, Lucien, along with fifty men, was in Oregon with Colonel Frémont's third expedition. Frémont, moving his men into California's Sacramento Valley, totally involved himself and at least some of his followers in war with the Californians and ended up in the middle of a competition for authority between Commodore Stockton and General Kearny. Eventually military troops escorted the Pathfinder back to the states, where he underwent court martial proceedings and resigned to enter civilian life.

Lucien was, if not in the battle itself, at the least a very close witness to that summer's takeover of Mexico's Pacific territory. More than a half million square miles, including what are now Arizona, New Mexico, and California, became part of the United States. Before young Lucien returned from his travels, Beaubien and Bent families paid the price for America's "bloodless" victory.

At the same time that western expansionism was capturing eastern imaginations, anti-western feeling was exploding in old New Mexico. Spanish and native New Mexicans vented growing ill will against their new government, their voices climaxing in dissent shortly after Kearny's departure from New Mexico toward California and it's military governorship.

In January 1847, after completion of Frémont's third expedition, Lucien was on his way home from Saint Louis. Waiting at Bent's Fort to accompany the next wagon train to Taos, he heard horrible news. Aroused by incendiary leaders, Pueblo Indians and Mexicans had risen in rebellion, killing "every American they could lay hands on."[25] Governor Charles Bent was dead. So was Lucien's brother-in-law, twenty-year-old Narciso, Carlos Beaubien's oldest child, having returned only a few weeks earlier from five years at Saint Mary's School. With every vestige of law and order shed, provisional government briefly stood terrorized and crumbling.

At Bent's Fort no one knew whether rebels had overcome troops at Santa Fe or even whether they themselves might be in danger. Everyone felt William Bent's grief for his murdered brother. The Cheyennes, eager to help their friend, proposed that their young warriors "march to Taos and scalp every Mexican." William declined the offer, and, because of the imminent possibility of attack, he remained at his fort while twenty-three men began an arduous wintertime trek across the mountains.[26]

Lucien Maxwell and Bill Bransford assumed leadership of the Bent's Fort contingent, three of whom beside Lucien had wives in Taos. After a week on the trail, they heard what sounded like thunder. Though it was a long way by road across the intervening mountains, only thirty-five or forty miles in actual distance separated them from Taos, and they quickly recognized sounds of battle. With their worst fears for their loved ones aroused, the men continued their dangerous journey into Mexican territory, land that might no longer be under American protection.[27]

They traveled for a month, worried about their families and battling heavy snow, leaving behind the towering Spanish Peaks and crossing Raton Pass onto the plains along the Canadian River. Finally they met up with one of George Bent's Indians on his way to the fort. From him they learned that Colonel Price had led two hundred fifty men into Taos and had succeeded in overpowering the Indians of Pueblo de Taos. They heard, too, of St. Vrain's quickly mustered collection of mountain men who contributed to defeat of the rebels. Maxwell and two others separated from the group, riding with all speed toward Taos where Luz was indeed safe, as were her parents and sisters. Narciso, he learned, had almost succeeded in hiding during the massacre, taking cover in an outhouse. A servant revealed Beaubien's son, bidding the rebels to, "Kill the young ones, and they will never be men to trouble us." Put to death and scalped, the young man had served the rebels' purposes as had Charles Bent and the other victims. The governor, although offered assistance by a Mexican woman, nevertheless was found and shot. With then tried to write some last message on paper that he carried in his pocket. Too weak, he could only offer quick prayers on their behalf before he fell, and the Indians surged into the room, quickly taking their enemy's gray scalp before departing in victory.[28]

Trials of the "traitors" followed, with Judges Carlos Beaubien and Charles Bent's friend, Joab Houghton, in charge of rendering "justice." Juries made up of Americans and sympathetic New Mexicans decided the rebels' fate, one of those jurors being Lucien Maxwell. George Bent served as the grand jury's foreman, and Elliott Lee, relative of the murdered sheriff, sat on the jury.[29] For fifteen days the court judged and sentenced. Executions followed in April. By summer it was over except, of course, for repercussions, which affected New Mexico long afterward.

The Treaty of Guadalupe Hidalgo was signed a year later by the United States and Mexico, then proclaimed in Washington, D.C. during the Fourth of July celebration of the nation's birthday. Meanwhile, bereaved families in Taos resumed their lives, Lucien working at his and James Quinn's store there. A time of healing commenced with the birth of a new son for Carlos and Pabla Beaubien, she then thirty-six years old. Surely grateful at their youngest and last child's August baptism, they must have welcomed even greater assuagement of their grief when their first grandchild was born the following April, Lucien and Luz's first child, Peter. The time had come for Beaubien to think again about settlement of his land grant.

He chose a location near the southern perimeter, where Rayado Creek watered a green valley, near where a well-traveled trail crossed eastward from the Santa Fe road over the mountain pass to Taos. Son-in-law Lucien led a small group of men to the site and supervised first the construction of temporary quarters made of logs and then preparation of timber for stronger, more lasting buildings. Early in the spring, Maxwell, along with a few of his men, departed for Kansas to purchase additional supplies.[30]

Although Rayado's construction proceeded without apparent difficulty, another problem delayed Lucien Maxwell's permanent settlement on the grant. As United States soldiers turned their attention toward war with Mexico, Indians renewed their resistance against wagon trains and settlers, their attacks in the northern New Mexico Territory more numerous than ever before.[31] Comanches, Kiowas, Pawnees, Namore numerous than ever before.[31] Comanches, Kiowas, Pawnees, Navajos, and Apaches all attacked. Only the Utes remained at peace during this time.[32] United States government agencies had yet to deal effectively with Indians already within its borders, much less manage forty thousand more, members of tribes roaming within New Mexican borders.

In June, when Lucien was returning from Bent's Fort to the new outpost at Rayado, Jicarilla Apaches wrought havoc on his pack train. A second attempt to cross the mountains through Manco Burro Pass met with even worse consequences. As the fourteen men and the two children, who were being taken to relatives in Taos, rested in the valley beneath high canyon walls and prepared to eat their noon meal, over a hundred Indians descended upon the group, chasing away their horses, surrounding the camp, and setting fire to the grass. After fighting for four hours, the eleven who had lived through the attack, eight of them injured, eventually retreated to the mountains. Elliott Lee wrote about the ensuing night, "Having lost every thing [sic] save what was on our backs, we suffered much from cold, and could not sleep."[33]

Fearful of further attack and traveling only at night, the men started for Taos, eighty miles away. Lucien Maxwell carried a bullet in his neck. Indian George, who had worked for George Bent until Bent's death the previous spring and now worked for Lucien, came to the aid of his new master, leaving cover to get water and carrying him on his back. Later, Lucien helped his servant in the same way, bringing water to the then wounded Indian George. Several days passed before a company of soldiers led by Dick Wootton, informed of the battle by friendly Indians, located Lucien and the others. With little clothing left and hardly able to walk, Lucien had suffered a large financial loss of thirty mules, fifty horses, and six hundred buckskins, a total of over seven thousand dollars.[34] But he was alive and able to celebrate his thirtieth birthday, very possibly with Luz and his infant son, Peter.

Unable to return to Rayado after surgical removal of the bullet in his neck, Lucien remained in Taos for one more winter. One day, during that winter, while at Beaubien's store with Dick Owens and Kit Carson, Lucien recognized a bearded stranger who staggered through the door. Neither Dick nor Kit realized the man was their old commander. Frémont, after failing to accomplish a winter crossing of the

San Juan Mountains, had found his way to Taos with Alexis Godey, a veteran of previous explorations. Ten of the forty-four men on this disastrous fourth expedition had already died. Kit and Lucien helped provide supplies, and Godey returned to rescue the desperate survivors.[35]

Staying at Kit's home until he recuperated, Frémont suggested that Kit accompany him to California. Kit, however, decided to remain with his friend Lucien, later saying to his biographer:

> In April, Mr. Maxwell and I concluded to make a settlement on the Rayado. We had been leading a roving life long enough and now was the time, if ever, to make a home for ourselves and children. We were getting old and could not expect to remain any length of time able to gain a livelihood as we had been such a number of years.[36]

While Lucien and Kit thought about settlement in northeastern New Mexico, word was already out about California's gold, discovered a year earlier and announced to the whole country in President Polk's farewell message to Congress. Swarms of people began their descent upon San Francisco, hoping for easy wealth to be retrieved from California streams, but neither Maxwell nor Carson found such pursuits to their liking.

Finally, in spring of 1849, Lucien Maxwell began permanent residence on the grant at the Rayado settlement situated in the northeastern part of what is now the state of New Mexico. Near a small river that maintained its flow throughout the year, Lucien's adobe house sat sheltered in a slight valley but close to a hill that provided an observation post. From there he could view both the Sangre de Cristos' rising slopes and the eastwardly stretching plains. It was an opportune time and place for a new settlement. With the Mexican War having ended, traffic on the Santa Fe Trail resumed; and wagons that took the mountain branch across Raton Pass traveled southward, their occupants happy indeed to find a place where a meal was cooked and served and they could sleep inside.

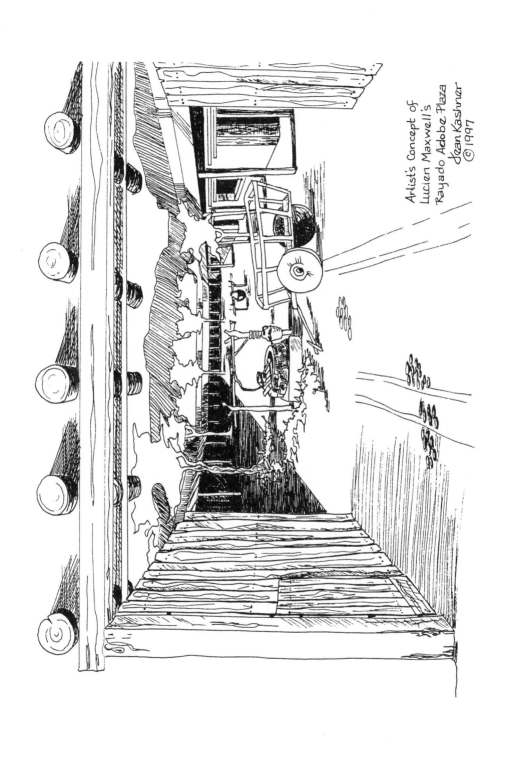

Artist's Concept of
Lucien Maxwell's
Rayado Adobe Plaza
Jean Kashner
© 1997

For a while, even with some few gold seekers taking the southern route to California, New Mexico remained a place apart from the rest of the country almost, but not quite, unchanged by comings and goings of opportunists who came only to take and then depart. Change did not happen as quickly in the Spanish culture that had been in existence for three hundred years. In comparison, America stretched and strained to keep up with its twenty million people and their push into new lands.

As Lucien Maxwell and Kit Carson settled down, everyone and everything else seemed to be in motion. The six-year-long financial depression came to an end as cross-country ventures increased and travelers needed and purchased supplies. The trail from Independence, Missouri, drew thousands of settlers westward to Oregon, and Brigham Young led the Latter Day Saints from Nauvoo, Illinois, to the Great Salt Lake in Utah.

In newly conquered California, cities sprang seemingly full-grown where two years earlier not even a lighthouse had dotted its shore and only ten thousand people had occupied the enormous coastal territory. In spite of General Kearny's attempts to honor the traditional Catholic society of the Mexican outpost, invading Yankees took over. A constant influx of those who sought only instant wealth destroyed the social and economic system that had previously developed among native-born Californians. Hundreds of immigrants arrived daily, one hundred thousand during 1849, more in one year than had come before in an entire decade. A constitutional convention of that year gathered forty-eight delegates in Monterey, only eight of whom were natives, representing thirteen thousand in a total population of one hundred thousand.[37]

And, back east, where they all came from, elections revealed growing political differences on the issue of slavery and the question of its extension into the new territories. Texas, Florida, Iowa, and Wisconsin joined the Union, evening the number of slave and free states. A third party pledged to free soil, free speech, free labor, and free men drew enough votes to split the Democratic party and win the presidency for General Zachary Taylor. The first women's rights convention gathered thirty-five women and thirty-two men in Seneca Falls, New York, to begin improving the conditions of wives.[38] While women began a quest which would ultimately win for them rights not only to inherit property but also to vote, business men discovered that the corporation could unite investors and also limit liability.

New machines modernized industry and commerce: telegraph lines, railroads, electric clocks, and bicycles. Scientists discovered ozone and men played in the first official baseball game. Americans read novels by Charlotte Brontë and Alexandre Dumas, as well as a new genre of literature, detective stories written by Edgar Allen Poe. Musicians played Verdi's music and the Astor Place Opera House opened in New York City with fifteen hundred seats.

At the same time, cities crowded more people into smaller areas where sewage and nonexistent waste disposal facilities resulted in indescribable filth. In many places, hogs scavenged garbage that urban residents heaved from buildings onto unpaved streets. Pedestrians in cities like Brooklyn, with a population of one hundred thousand, often had to yield to herds of cows or pigs being led along city avenues to and from nearby farms and meadows.[39] America, in its youth, was only beginning to learn about itself, about reconciling its needs with its desires, its ideals with reality, states rights with federal government.

Moving its Bureau of Indian Affairs from the Department of War to the Department of the Interior, the United States of America took its first step toward inclusion of the Indian Nations in a relationship other than military. Hardly able to deal with natives of occupied lands, Americans found that their new democracy was attracting immigrants from across the ocean. With annual debarkation of three hundred thousand persons, diversity arrived with "aliens" from Ireland and Germany and dissatisfied escapees from revolutions in France, Italy, and Germany, where a rising middle class was demanding a voice in government. New ideas about religion pervaded society. Spiritualism, mysticism, harmonialism, mesmerism, and perfectionism offered explanations and comfort in the face of overwhelming change. And newly opened territories appealed to both the adventurous and the desperate.

Opportunists came to make their fortunes and return to civilization; but some individuals found a new world west of the Mississippi, a world where they could be part of establishing the rules, where what a man or woman did to take care of himself meant the difference between survival and death.

As broadening westward trails interspersed prairies and mountain passes, Lucien Maxwell decided, for better and for worse, definitely for richer, rather than poorer, to remain in New Mexico, at least in his mind at that time, until death did him part. There, he could work in the two things he knew best, agriculture and business. Thirty years old, husband and father, he was undeterred from that point on in his resolution to make himself a place. As both friends and enemies agreed when describing him in later years, Mac "was a man that nothing in the world would prevent him from accomplishing what he undertook to do, in fact, no one ever dared to . . . stand in the way of anything that he started out to accomplish."[40]

As Lucien Maxwell optimistically began his twenty years in Cimarron country, another westerner's dream was coming to an end. William Bent, forty years old, despaired. Already beset by losses of not only his wife, but also his three brothers, he faced another ending when his long-time partner Ceran St. Vrain separated from the company. Then a cholera epidemic swept through his people's camps, half of the southern Cheyennes falling in its wake. On August 21, 1849, facing destruction of all the fairness he had achieved in dealings with Indians and Whites alike, William Bent set a torch to the fort that carried his name and left its smoldering embers as evidence of the end of an era.[41]

Lucien, protected by his youth, could hardly have foreseen that he, too, would experience a similar sense of hopelessness in the face of inevitable change. How could he have known that, twenty years in the future, when both Kit Carson and William Bent were dead, he would walk away from his own creation and contribution to the west, his home on the Cimarron, just one hundred fifty miles southwest of the old Bent's Fort?

4

RAYADO
1850 TO 1859

As thousands headed into Oregon country, taking advantage of the government's free land offer, hundreds of thousands sought gold in California. Santa Fe Trail ruts widened and deepened, wheels of commerce continuing to roll. Having left anything resembling a residence months and many miles behind, travelers knew or quickly learned, following their southerly descent from Raton Pass, they were on the Beaubien grant. Maxwell's home was only days away. They saw, on the western horizon, towering snowcapped peaks and crossed first the Vermejo River and then the Cimarron, rivers that, if the previous winter's snowfall had been heavy, offered a cool drink for animals and humans alike. They watched in awe, understanding the name given the southern range of the Rocky Mountains, as the sunset glowed in reddish tints on the Sangre de Cristo Mountains. It was indeed as though the "Blood of Christ" had spread upon them.

First timers couldn't help but notice the quickening pace of oxen or mules as they approached what is now the Rayado River. As they descended a slight incline, the trail made a final turn, revealing the expansive, one-story structure, its inner courtyard providing a shady retreat from intense afternoon sun and cloudless blue skies. There, where never-ending high plains abutted sheer mountain walls, herds of cattle and horses grazed on sweet-smelling grass. Flowing from natural springs that broke free from the earth's crust thousands of feet above and gathered currents from melting snow, cool water offered relief from summer's excruciatingly dry heat. Back in Illinois, folks called such trickles of water creeks, but in New Mexico, water that flowed all year was a river, a blessed gift.

Beaubien and Miranda had chosen well. Most of New Mexico's sixty-one thousand Spaniards and Mestizos lived on the other side of the Sangre de Cristo Mountains, along the Rio Grande. Here, on its eastern slopes, Jicarilla Apaches and Mouache Utes hunted in mountain forests during summer months, then wintered along the rivers in sheltered valleys. Though their numbers had greatly decreased since Spaniards first sought gold in North America, the Indians nevertheless had maintained their culture and survived. New Mexico had a few more years of grace before exploitation of its mountains and forests began. A population that had existed in the Mexican territory's remote northern inland did not quickly change, but it did appreciate trade. And the traders welcomed a stopping place at Rayado.

There, at the southernmost point of Beaubien and Miranda's grant, the trail to Taos turned westward and continued thirty miles over the pass. Wagons headed for Santa Fe, too ponderous and heavy for the shorter route, had to travel southward another one hundred fifty miles, around the mountains and finally northward to Santa Fe. There, at Rayado, Lucien Maxwell built his first home, where Luz, two-year-old Peter, and baby Virginia could join him in safety and some degree of comfort, beside a rising hill that offered shelter from winds and storms, where trees grew and summer breezes cooled its rooms.

From the beginning of his residence in New Mexico's unsettled territory, Lucien exemplified his Illinois family's tradition of hospitality, welcoming all travelers into his home; and, from the beginning, he adapted to his surroundings. Most of the other Americans in the area sought to Christianize and modernize. With narrow military vision, newcomers attempted to make the conquered country "American," but Lucien, in his own way, blended the two cultures. Utilizing both adobe and wood, he built a home in the Mexican adobe tradition with the rooms of the home and its walls surrounding an inner patio. Recognizing what land required of people who lived on it, Lucien revealed a unique attitude that established a sound basis for all his future endeavors.

In the complex, containing multiple buildings and surrounded by high adobe walls, Lucien's sixteen-to-twenty-room house allowed ample space for a growing family. Occupying an acre of land, its open, middle area extended rectangularly approximately one hundred eighty by two hundred feet.[1] Several hundred feet southeast of Lucien's house, Kit Carson lived with his family in another adobe residence. In addition to Lucien, with his French and Irish background, and Carson's Scotch-Irish, American pioneer stock, were Zan Hicklin from Holland; Jesse Nelson from Scandinavia; Mexican Jesús Silva; Lucien's wife, French and Spanish; Carson's wife, purely Spanish; Josepha's young niece, Teresina Bent of English and Spanish ancestry; and Carson's daughter Adaline, by his Indian wife. In a blending of diverse roots, "the colony represented the American frontier in the southwest."[2] Fifteen to twenty families planted and harvested crops, herded cattle and sheep, and generally prospered. Lucien's leadership united them all in his plans for Beaubien and Miranda's grant. Although Lucien was interested in making his *rancho* a place of comfort and some elegance, social differences blended in a new way. One visitor from east of the Mississippi observed that Mexicans, Americans, and Indians all sat together for meals at the same table.[3]

Rayado grew rapidly, especially after the government established a military post there. Under orders to protect the Santa Fe Trail from attacking plains Indians, some forty-three soldiers moved into the first building constructed. Though the post existed only a little more than a year, it permitted the small community to take root. Lucien's well-thought-out irrigation provided hay for troops' horses as well as grazing acreage for surplus government livestock. New families arrived, taking advantage of Beaubien and Maxwell's profit-sharing arrangements whereby they received cattle and land in exchange for a percentage of proceeds.[4] Along with lucrative markets for goods brought in from Missouri, stables and quarters brought in rents of three thousand four hundred dollars per year and provided employment opportunities for several men and women. Six hundred tons of hay at thirty dollars per ton helped provide sufficient profit for the settlement's survival.[5] Each small success opened the way for the next and larger one.

Lucien's previous Manco Burro Pass injuries and loss of money had depleted his assets, but Rayado's settlement replenished his resources. As Carson said, they "were in a way of becoming prosperous."[6] Lucien Maxwell, having grown up on Illinois and Missouri farmland, recognized the grazing potential in New Mexico's high country grass.

Grama cured on the ground and provided excellent hay all winter long, thus not requiring labor intensive feeding of stock.[7] Gradually increasing herds of livestock, along with additional construction, fostered Rayado's growth.

Because of construction of Fort Union, forty miles south of Rayado, permanent military presence on the grant ceased; but Kit Carson, as purchasing agent for the area's Utes and Apaches, made good use of Rayado's harvests in supplying them with rations.[8] He and Lucien managed quite well, marketing produce; stocking and selling manufactured goods, calico and flannel cloth, axes, knives, and farm tools; making enough profit to buy what they in turn needed. As Rayado's small group of men and women plowed and harvested, their settlement east of the Sangre de Cristo Mountains remained somewhat isolated, particularly from political processes that involved New Mexico's territorial status. California became a state and the Texas border was determined; but New Mexico remained a territory for the next sixty years, a pawn in United States attempts at reconciliation of bickering sectional interests and arguments over extension of slavery. "Carson and Maxwell passed politics up in favor of straight business."[9]

While the rest of the country rushed to California seeking gold, thirty-five-year-old Lucien Maxwell had found his niche, intending to do more with his life than striking it rich with a pick and shovel or a pan in a stream. Whether he started out to rule an empire or whether, as a bright and enterprising individual, he was merely caught up in his country's history can be argued from either side; but land in new territories was definitely an old family goal. By the time Lucien was entertaining visitors at Rayado, his cousin Michel had already carried the Menard tradition to Texas. In Galveston, the man who had married Lucien's older sister also primarily occupied himself with business endeavors and had established himself as one of the city's founders. Fellow Texans described him as a powerful man who spoke with "a strong French accent, which he never lost, and his animated gestures added to the charm of his conversation." Like Lucien, he "dispensed lavish hospitality to his white and Indian friends."[10]

The family pattern was there and Lucien, too, chose a new path into unsettled country. Rayado was a first step on that path. As Armijo had known when he allocated land in northeastern New Mexico, Americans were willing to move into Indian territory where every day was a risk. But not all Americans could accomplish what Lucien did. A community could not be built without people. Only the most determined and able men were able to foster a feeling of safety and economic opportunity that encouraged others to share pioneering's trouble as well as its profits. The fact that Rayado thrived proves Lucien Maxwell's ability to do just that, its families depending upon his ability to get them through difficult times, those who joined him putting their own and their families' lives on the line. In spite of their isolation from Washington and even from Santa Fe, families, herds, and profits multiplied.

With life going so smoothly, Lucien and Kit "determined on having one more old-fashioned beaver hunt, such as they were accustomed to a score of years before." Choosing a very dangerous route, they gathered several former compatriots and started out on the South Fork of the Platte, completed a circular route to the Arkansas River, and then returned home. Their trapping excursion lasted several weeks and actually found a replenished animal population in the northern mountains.[11]

Heavy winter snows lingered into spring of the next year. "The snow was so deep on the west side of the Sangre de Cristo Pass" that in February a group of settlers "traveled only ten miles in eight days. At the top they spent another day stamping a path through a mammoth drift that lay across the trail."[12] That was the spring that Carson, then forty-three years old, and Lucien, nine years younger, departed on another adventure; this one, however, to make money. Lucien followed Dick Wootton and Kit Carson north to Wyoming and west to Sacramento. Each man, along with a small group of herders, led thousands of sheep to the burgeoning population of gold seekers in California. Grazing and moving several thousand sheep that distance was no small task, but the several-month-long trip was worth the effort. Uncle Dick returned to the Arkansas valley with fourteen thousand dollars in gold and "more than twice as much more in drafts on Saint Louis," a profit of over ten times what the sheep had cost him. Selling their animals at between two and five dollars per head, Kit and Lucien also pocketed substantial sums.[13]

Once they reached Sacramento and sold their animals, Carson and Maxwell returned to what had been the sparsely inhabited lands they had seen when working with Frémont seven years earlier. California had changed dramatically. The old village of Yerba Buena, with less than a hundred residents, had become San Francisco, financial center of the new state where Henry Wells offered one hundred dollar shares and raised three hundred thousand dollars to start the Wells Fargo Corporation. It transported millions of dollars in gold back east, but plenty remained, visible in "six hundred new brick and stone buildings, a hundred sixty hotels and boardinghouses, sixty-six restaurants and twenty bathing houses. The city's waterfront lots, twenty-five feet wide and sixty feet deep, now sold for ten thousand dollars each."

Lucien traveled by steamer down the coast to Los Angeles, arriving two weeks earlier than Carson, who didn't want to undergo another ocean passage. Los Angeles, "in contrast to San Francisco, was achieving neither boom nor bust. There were fugitive signs of growth in 1852; the city had started a harbor at San Pedro, sixteen to twenty miles away. . . . The town could boast no more than a chapel facing the Plaza, and fifty buildings, with half a dozen of them two-storied, placed like cardboard boxes on a treeless, flowerless, shadeless baking semi-desert plain."[14]

Lucien probably felt at home in rural and desert-like Los Angeles. Arriving at the harbor, then San Pedro Bay, visitors rode in a horse-drawn coach up to the plaza. Facing the small open area, the Catholic church's bell tower rose above unevenly clustered adobe houses that lined winding, crowded streets. Even the village's wealthiest residents in the few two-storied buildings looked upward toward the church's wooden cross. "Roadways seemed to grope aimlessly through town looking for an exit to the nearby valleys." Americans in Los Angeles numbered only three hundred of the city's four thousand residents and a county Indian population of another four thousand. Amid the diverse jumble of races and nationalities, Yankees had to learn Mexican ways of doing business, and getting along with neighbors called for more than cash.[15]

With a full taste of what gold could do to a place that had been so hospitable and lovely, Carson and Maxwell left, glad to be returning home and rewarded for their labor with heavy bankrolls. Across Arizona they traveled, arriving back in Taos on Christmas Day 1853.[16] Carson had been appointed Indian Agent, a job which required his moving to Taos. Both Carson and Maxwell spent the next few years dealing with Indian troubles, Lucien particularly affected by the Utes and Apaches who shared Beaubien and Miranda's land.

As mountain men, the two friends had established relationships with individuals of various Indian nations, learning and teaching at the same time, achieving a unique understanding of "savages." Certainly they had killed rather than be killed, but they learned quickly about the value of a friend, be that friend Indian or white. Kit Carson and Lucien Maxwell knew about costs of survival, about being without food, water, and horses; and such knowledge placed them on an equal footing with Indians. Above all, they knew the importance of keeping one's word, and that seemed to be the one thing their government remained unable to accomplish.

United States Indian policy was at best inconsistent and unreliable, set forth by a government unwilling to keep its word. Congress twenty years earlier had created a supposedly permanent boundary between Indian and United States land, a boundary to be supervised and enforced by the American military.[17] Only licensed travelers could trade west of the Mississippi, except in Missouri and Louisiana. Within two years of that pronouncement defining Indian country, the permanent line changed to accommodate settlers and miners in Iowa and Wisconsin territories. Then again, at the conclusion of United States war with Mexico, territory added west and south of Indian country erased former agreements. Kansas and Nebraska spread westerly across land where plains Indians hunted buffalo, and occupation of Minnesota pushed from the north. The United States government had given its solemn word, acknowledged its obligation to honor treaties that prescribed boundaries of Indian territory; but it never addressed the problem of its citizens pouring into other people's lands, United States citizens insisting that those other people learn to live like white men.

Records of treaty after treaty fill Washington archives, each promising lasting peace. In 1851 a treaty signed at Fort Laramie granted permission for roads and military posts across northern plains, thus acknowledging tribal ownership of lands. Cheyennes, Arapahos, Sioux, and Crows agreed to tribal boundaries that included what is now eastern Colorado, western Kansas, parts of southern Nebraska, and Wyoming. Nothing, however, prevented a growing number of squatters from erecting shacks in a place eventually to be known as Denver.

In New Mexico, where the Treaty of Guadalupe Hidalgo five years earlier had ended hostilities between the United States and Mexico, a population estimate of sixty thousand did not include Utes, Apaches and Navajos; but General Kearny promised to protect conquered Mexicans from their Indian enemies. Attempting to make peace with the Indians, Kearny resorted to other promises that he could not keep. Resulting misunderstandings underscored Washington's typically inept and absentee handling of Indian affairs. The Mexican Colonization Law of 1828, with its express provision for continued Indian residency until such time that they voluntarily determined to leave, remained unrecognized by the United States under its 1848 treaty with Mexico.[18]

In the first treaty with the Ute Indian Nation that occupied what is now eastern Utah, northern New Mexico, and most of Colorado, no boundaries were established; but the United States government guaranteed the "People of the Shining Mountains" an annual compensation of five thousand dollars in exchange for assurance of safe passage through Ute territory.

"For over four years the Utes kept their side of the bargain. . . . Peace with the white man was bought at great cost to themselves. As the hostile Indians of New Mexico made off with cattle, sheep, horses, guns and clothing, goods and captives, the Utes grew poorer and poorer, lacking even guns and ammunition to kill game. Not a penny of the `donations and presents' promised them in the treaty of 1849 had been distributed as late as August 1852. No Indian agent had been stationed among them."[19]

Jicarilla Apaches also signed a treaty in which they recognized United States authority; agreed to specified boundaries; and declared their intent to farm, to call a halt to attacks against Americans, and to give up property and captives seized during such aggressions. Their immediate compliance was not matched on the part of their new government since promised merchandise, money, and tools that would permit their attempting to farm the land could not be forthcoming until the treaty was ratified. The Indians, in the meantime, had to remain outside a fifty-mile radius of any town or road. Such unreasonable expectations led only to further turmoil. Then, when Congress did not ratify the Treaty of 1851, once again, misunderstanding caused even more conflict.[20]

Repeating change of command in the United States hierarchy left decision making with the inexperienced. Open hostilities broke out. The military believed the only remedy to be a full show of strength on behalf of the United States government, and a state of war continued through 1855 when all parties came together to agree upon yet another treaty. Under its conditions, Jicarillas exchanged their claim to all lands for a prescribed reservation and bimonthly delivery of provisions and annuities. Again, Congress refused to ratify the treaty.[21]

During all this time, settlers in northeastern New Mexico faced frontier life's reality, coping as best they could with thefts of livestock and threats to their very lives. Angry invading Indians had no way to understand powerless white chiefs whose promises never resulted in action from their government. In the spring of 1854, a Santa Fe newspaper reported that Indians had murdered Maxwell and all of Rayado's inhabitants.[22] But the group of families had not succumbed, though for a few months during the following summer troops once again occupied the little settlement. Rayado men and women stuck out the hard times and arrived at their own relationship with neighboring Indians.

Settling was hard. Indians and ineptitude of United States government officials made it harder. Men and women had to plant and plow and grow food; herd cattle, sheep, and horses; and tend to all the usual problems of raising families in a place far removed from any assistance, medical or otherwise. Their leader had to know not only the land and the benefits it offered, but also the difficulties it mounted: winter snows and summer droughts; grizzlies, rattlesnakes, tarantulas; and always, always, the unexpected. Lucien Maxwell was the one upon whom they depended to effect their survival in the face of most critical situations.

Profit from his California trip permitted Lucien to further develop agricultural and mercantile enterprises and to make his and Luz's enlarging family comfortable in their Rayado home. Their house was, according to Kit Carson's first biographer, in the middle of a green valley the likes of which were only to be found on well-watered spots at the base of mountains. Lush grassy fields extended from both banks of the river, creating a picturesque backdrop for the city-block-sized struc-

ture where the Maxwells resided. With its spacious rooms, center courtyard, and surrounding porch, the homeplace provided luxury previously unimagined for that part of the country. Along with the
settlement's several buildings and productive meadows, Rayado clearly
demonstrated the owner's "honest pride" in "being the master of a model
farm."[23] Fifteen thousand head of cattle grazed under his auspices and
over two hundred acres were under cultivation.[24]

Time had now come for Carlos Beaubien to begin the expensive
and lengthy procedure of having his grant confirmed under United States
law. Although the treaty which ended war with Mexico promised recognition of previous ownership under Mexican law, eight years passed
before the United States government turned its attention to New Mexico.
As one of the first of over a thousand claimants, Beaubien accomplished
early confirmation of not only the Beaubien and Miranda Grant but also
the Sangre de Cristo lands he had inherited from his murdered son. In
September, shortly after Lucien's thirty-ninth birthday, first Surveyor
General of New Mexico William Pelham validated Beaubien's claim,
recommending congressional acceptance.

For Lucien, one success followed another. Receiving a letter from
Guadalupe Miranda about sale of his interest in their grant, Beaubien
passed the opportunity on to his son-in-law; and in April, Lucien Maxwell purchased in its entirety all rights and full title to Miranda's portion for two thousand five hundred dollars, paying an additional two
hundred forty-five dollars to Beaubien for half his legal fees.[25]

Now a major landowner, he organized plans for a bigger house
and more meadows for enlarging numbers of horses, cattle, and sheep.
Work began at a site eleven miles north, where the Santa Fe Trail crossed
the Cimarron River. Either while their new home's construction was
under way or soon after its completion, Maxwell decided to visit
Kaskaskia. Ten-year-old Peter now had four younger sisters: Virginia,
age eight; Emilia, age six; Sofia, age four; and Maria, almost two. Though
there was stage service between Santa Fe and Independence, Missouri,
which took about two weeks, Luz would have been more comfortable
traveling at a slower speed in the family's wagons and Concord coaches.

Usually red, green, or yellow, these large wooden vehicles, their
frames reinforced with iron, could carry two tons; pulled by six horses,
each one cost fourteen hundred dollars and itself weighed more than a

ton. Six to nine travelers could ride inside and that many more on top. Leather straps called thorough braces suspended the coach's solid hardwood body over the frame, creating a continuous rocking motion for all passengers, and ironclad wooden wheels withstood the brunt of contact with mud and rocks.[26]

The entire family traveled east. Leaving New Mexico's arid high altitude, traveling across level, grassy plains, viewing vast herds of bison, then leaving the Missouri River and the city of Westport, the family finally reached the Mississippi. The depth and force of its waters astounded people who had known only the Rio Grande and Cimarron's summer-subsiding flows and so, too, on the river's eastern side, oak trees so huge that their limbs shaded several wagons. Arrival of Lucien and his entourage must have been something of an event in Kaskaskia. Lucien, no longer an Illinoisan, returned to his childhood in the quiet, past-its-zenith town of Kaskaskia, Illinois, with not only twenty years as a seasoned and experienced westerner, but also with stature as a landowner of extensive acreage. Back in New Mexico, on the day of his fortieth birthday, he had become majority partner in the Beaubien and Miranda Grant. Carlos and Pabla Beaubien transferred Rayado's title to Lucien, for a nominal price of only five hundred dollars. A few years earlier Lucien had purchased a one-sixth interest in Beaubien's Sangre de Cristo Grant for that same amount. He and his family were thriving.

As East and West came together for a brief moment in Kaskaskia, the rest of the nation was splitting farther apart. A Supreme Court decision in the Dred Scott case and the Kansas-Nebraska Act erased the Missouri Compromise and effectively removed any hope for resolution of territorial slavery issues. There in Illinois, while Lucien and his family were visiting, two men debated, campaigning for votes in the coming election of that state's senator. National issues made headlines as the Western Union Telegraph Company sent their words to newspapers around the country.

"A house divided against itself cannot stand," said Abe Lincoln, only ten years older than Lucien and already a seasoned legislator in the House of Representatives. Two years earlier Lincoln had joined the new antislavery Republican party and strongly supported its candidate for president, Lucien's former employer, John C. Frémont. Two years later, Abe Lincoln was himself the presidential candidate and first Republican to achieve the nation's highest office.

Slowly and surely sectional division magnified, with slavery representing all cultural and economic differences between southern agrarians and northern industrialists. Competition for political power centered upon whether North or South would control western territories. Southern resentment festered against a growing northern population that refused to recognize slaveholders' property rights and the very institution that had created wealth and power in the south. Disputes between individuals and government remained unresolved.

As autumn colored the trees in Kaskaskia, and cold winds from the west crossed the river to find them, the family prepared to return home, but not before Kaskaskia's cemetery claimed yet one more of Lucien Maxwell's loved ones. Maria's death at the end of October, a month and a half before her second birthday, must have affected them all. Luz, not yet thirty years old, must have been overwhelmed by her trip east, meeting her husband's family, being in a strange place where very few people spoke Spanish and where she lost her youngest child. Doleful calls of wolves during the long nights of their journey home echoed the family's sadness.

What they had anticipated being a quiet and uneventful return to New Mexico instead witnessed an explosion of gold fever. The decade that had begun with hordes rushing to California ended with a mass ascent to Colorado and Nevada. Prospectors rushed by the thousands to new finds, like locusts to a field of wheat, to Colorado, to Utah, and to Nevada's Comstock Lode.

> *There were hardly facilities to take care of a hundred newcomers, let alone a hundred thousand. The name "Colorado" had not yet officially emerged, eastern headlines read: "GOLD IN KANSAS TERRITORY !!! THE PIKE'S PEAK'S MINES !!!." . . . Onto the banks of the Missouri River they came from every state in the east and midwest. They came by steamboat, on horseback and muleback and on foot, with knapsacks over one shoulder and rifles over the other; a young crowd, under thirty, as were the California Argonauts, described as having "light hearts and a thin pair of*

breeches," having left behind their jobs, homes, wives, chil-
dren, many of them setting out across the Kansas prairies for
the eight-hundred-mile trek with no more than a week's pro-
visions.[27]

Rough mining shacks at the Rocky Mountains' eastern edge became towns where men whom Lucien knew well started businesses.
Uncle Dick Wootton made a quick profit when he drove into Denver
with a wagon load of whiskey and goods, but his store quickly failed.
J.B. Doyle and Company was more successful, becoming "the largest
mercantile firm in the territory. It did half a million dollars' worth of
business a year and had branches at Cānon City, Pueblo, Tarryall
(Fairplay), and other mining camps in the mountains."[28] Settlers in
Carson Valley, unsuccessful seven years earlier in making Nevada an
independent territory, sent their delegate to Washington with visible
proof of Nevada's wealth: a one hundred thirty-pound piece of rich
Comstock ore.[29]

The Southwest was becoming American territory, but optimistic gold seekers paid little attention to news that had nothing to do with
their picks and shovels. Minnesota and Oregon became states and President James Buchanan stood helpless in the face of broadening division
between North and South. While Czar Alexander II emancipated Rus-
sian serfs, the United States was about to deal with its slavery problems
in a different way. While Louis Pasteur, Joseph Lister, and Robert Koch
made strides against disease, Darwin's *Origin of the Species* and Karl
Marx' *Das Kapital* created an uproar. A changing country in a changing
world was leaving behind its childhood's agrarian roots.

Lucien Maxwell's home on the mountain branch of the Santa
Fe Trail stands like a last beacon on the horizon of the old west. He
learned a style of leadership from the very people with whom he shared
his land. "The Jicarillas shared a common culture, but not an overall
formal political organization. The independent and autonomous political units had leaders, influential persons who acquired their positions
through skill and wisdom. Each local group had a leader who represented the interests of his followers. It was his responsibility to negoti-
ate disputes with neighboring groups over matters of territory or re-
venge, and he arbitrated internal conflicts. Having no absolute author-

ity, these leaders governed by persuasion, and their powers were only as great as their abilities to act in the capacity of advocate and to achieve a consensus and promote peaceful coexistence. Leaders gained their positions on the basis of their accomplishments and generosity."[30]

Ultimately, even experienced mountain man Lucien Maxwell was forced to admit defeat in his personal struggle to live side by side with the thousand Mouache Utes and Jicarilla Apaches who also occupied the Beaubien and Miranda Grant and called its forests their home. "Pike's Peak or Bust" rang out across the country and echoed ominously southward. Gold had brought the Spaniards and now its glittering allure magnetized the Americans.

5

CIMARRON
1860 TO 1869

> . . . *commencing below the junction of the Rayado River with*
> *the Colorado, and in a direct line towards the east to the first*
> *hills, and from there running parallel with said River Colo-*
> *rado in a northerly direction to opposite the point of the Uña*
> *de Gato, following the same river along the same hills, to con-*
> *tinue to the east of said Uña de Gato River to the summit of*
> *the table-land (mesa); from whence turning northwest, to fol-*
> *low along said summit until it reaches the top of the moun-*
> *tain which divides the waters of the rivers running towards*
> *the east from those running towards the west, and from thence,*
> *following the line of said mountain in a southwardly direc-*
> *tion, until it intersects the first hill south of the Rayado River,*
> *and following the summit of said hill toward the east to the*
> *place of beginning.*
>
> Beaubien and Miranda Land Grant
> Requested of the Mexican government
> January 8, 1841[1]

Today's travelers, driving from Denver to Santa Fe via an inter-
state highway, are not aware that, from Trinidad, south to Springer,
and west to the top of the "shining mountains" at the farthest point of
their vision, almost all the land was part of a Mexican land grant originally awarded to Carlos Beaubien and Guadalupe Miranda in 1841. Visi-

tors to Cimarron, New Mexico, at the close of the twentieth century, have little conception of the man who was responsible for growth of a thriving trade center one hundred fifty years ago. Lucien Maxwell, though he developed, fought for, and managed it for twenty years, was actual owner, along with his wife Luz, of the entire grant for only a few months.

In June 1860, Congress confirmed the Beaubien and Miranda Grant. A few years earlier, engaging competent legal counsel, Beaubien had filed appropriate papers with New Mexico's Surveyor General and subsequently received acknowledgement that the grant was good.

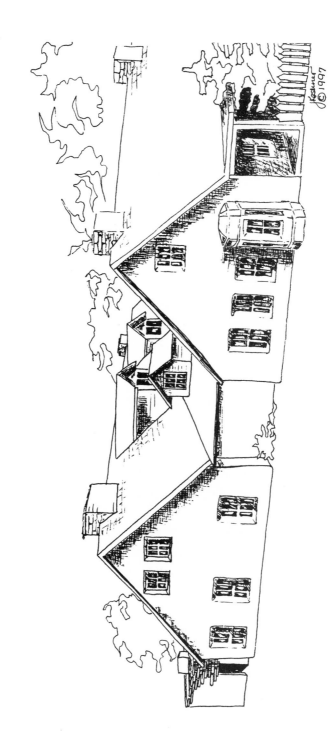

Home of Lucian and Luz Maxwell, Cimarron, New Mexico

Beaubien's lands were among the first of the New Mexican land grants to be recognized. Unlike in California, where the mechanism for making claim was stipulated and acted upon promptly by the Federal Government, quite the opposite situation existed in New Mexico. Claimants had to bear the large expense of investigation and survey. The process, sketchy at best and expensive at a time when money was very scarce, caused many to delay out of fear of dispossession and, because of their inaction, eventually separated long-time residents from their lands. Congressional inattention resulted in questions about titles and boundaries, issues that lingered in federal courts long after Beaubien's death.

But such problems lay ahead and far out of sight. In the meantime, as the decade began, Lucien approached his forty-second birthday, his and Luz's new home built alongside the Cimarron River a center of activity in northeastern New Mexico. The two-story, white-washed, adobe structure had three-foot-thick walls and surrounded an open court. A covered porch extended along its entire eastern length.[2]

Though it looked very American from the outside, much like the houses of Kaskaskia and Sainte Genevieve, courtyards in the Mexican style joined three separate sections. A hundred yards or so on the south side of the river and high enough to prevent flooding, the house stood sheltered from the view of never-ending plains by a small hill that rose to the east; tall trees growing between it and the river offered protection from winter's northerly winds. Lucien could stand on his porch and observe everything that was going on in the square-like area of the growing town. A few hundred yards to the west a sturdy barn stored supplies and feed; farther west and in its first stages of construction rose a three-story grist mill that required three years to build. Just a few miles farther away, towering abruptly on the western horizon, Sangre de Cristo peaks abutted the sky. Lucien could watch serene blue sky disappear when summer storms blew heavy, black clouds over the mountains and brought long, rolling thunder that echoed through the river's canyon as much-needed rain descended into the valley. In winter, he could watch the sun vanish into silent whiteness as snow spread across the high country.

Aztec Mill, Cimarron, New Mexico

Two years had passed since little Maria's death during the family's visit to Kaskaskia and the August birth of another daughter seemed auspicious for the family's future happiness. Twelve-year-old Peter and his younger sisters, ages ten, eight, and six, welcomed their new sibling who was named Verenisa. Increasing numbers of travelers on the mountain branch of the Santa Fe Trail appreciated Lucien's hospitality. Life was good. And for a short while it seemed that it could continue so.

Colonel Henry Inman, assistant quartermaster at nearby Fort Union, knew Lucien after the former mountain man had become a middle-aged entrepreneur, established in reputation and settled in wealth and comfort on a vast acreage, a man content with his own sense of who and what he was. Inman described Lucien like a character from an English novel:

> At the zenith of his influence and wealth, during the War of the Rebellion, when New Mexico was isolated and almost independent of care or thought by the government at Washington, he lived in a sort of barbaric splendour[sic], akin to that of the nobles of England at the time of the Norman conquest.
>
> The thousands of arable acres comprised in the many fertile valleys of his immense estate were farmed in a primitive, feudal sort of way, by native Mexicans principally, under the system of peonage then existing in the Territory. He employed about five hundred men, and they were as much his thralls as were Gurth and Wamba of Cedric of Rotherwood, only they wore no engraved collars around their necks bearing their names and that of their master. Maxwell was not a hard governor and his people really loved him, as he was ever their friend and adviser.
>
> His house was a palace when compared with the prevailing style of architecture in that country, and cost an immense sum of money. It was large and roomy, purely American in its construction, but the manner of conducting it was strictly Mexican, varying between the customs of the higher and lower classes of that curious people.[3]

Indeed, the Maxwell home must have seemed like a palace in comparison to Inman's rough army quarters at Fort Union and also for all travelers on the Santa Fe Trail's mountain route. From Bent's Fort, hundreds of miles and many days to the east, they saw nothing of meals served at a table, nor did they sleep under a roof. After travel across hot, windswept plains, then undergoing the difficult ascent over Raton Pass, they probably cheered with joy at the site of the American looking, two-story house on the hill rising from the river's edge.

In addition to its location on the Santa Fe Trail and the major road linking Taos and Bent's Fort, Lucien's Cimarron house connected east and west through its supplies for daily stages run by the Overland Mail. Nine passengers rode inside and two outside with the driver, for two hundred fifty dollars each and an extra fifty cents per pound for baggage exceeding forty pounds. The fare "included the board of the travelers, but they were not catered to in any extravagant manner; hardtack, bacon, and coffee usually exhausted the menu, save that at times there was an abundance of antelope and buffalo."[4]

Stagecoach passengers slept and sat in the same position during the two weeks they traveled from the Missouri River to Santa Fe. They camped at night, gathering buffalo-chips for fires on which to boil coffee or cook buffalo steak. During the decade's early years, friendly Indians invited travelers into their villages, entertaining them with music and a meal of venison or buffalo. Crossing the treeless plains, coaches often journeyed from morning until evening through herds of buffalo, covering a hundred miles before leaving them behind. With one set of mules hauling the coach, they could make the lonely two hundred forty miles between Fort Larned and Fort Lyon in four or five days, if the weather was good. Winter trips usually met sideward blowing snow and frigid temperatures on the ascending western plains.[5]

Lucien welcomed everyone to his beautiful home at the center of a busy community that boasted a post office and a major stageline stop. Wagons and coaches crossed the river at the Cimarron ford, their passengers usually taking advantage of Maxwell hospitality. Two dining rooms, one for men and one for women, with tables set "daily for about thirty persons" were tended by "a retinue of servants."[6] Some people offered to pay for room and board only to be told sternly by their host, "I don't keep hotel."[7]

Cimarron was home to the hundreds of people who made their livelihood on the grant's lands. New Mexico's particular nuances of employment differed considerably from eastern standards. Though many residents on the Beaubien and Miranda Grant did not own their land, they were not slaves, but instead turned over a portion of their produce and herds to their *patron*. In addition to herdsmen and farmers, "at all times, and in all seasons, the group of buildings, houses, stables, mill, store, and their surrounding grounds, were a constant resort and loafing-place of Indians."[8] Everyone submitted to, and most welcomed, Lucien's leadership, the price exacted for having laws and rules in their lives. New Mexico's northeastern corner was wilderness. The law was made by those willing to enforce it.

Inevitably, even as Cimarron's families found tranquillity and prosperity, events east of the Mississippi stirred differences between North and South to an explosive climax. In November 1860, meteor showers above Manhattan mirrored results of elections for sixteenth president of the United States. Thirty-three stars on the American flag, representing a population of thirty-one million, split asunder. Abe Lincoln, one of four candidates, stood firmly against slavery; and though the combined popular vote went against him, he carried enough states to win the electoral vote. By the time he was sworn in as president, just fifty-two years old, seven southern states had seceded from the Union and the Confederacy had selected Jefferson Davis to be its president. The following year Kansas attained statehood and Colorado, territorial status. Sectionalism that had been held in check by Congress and the young expanding country's succeeding presidents could no longer be shunted aside. A strong central government had to take control of the country, and northern industrialists seized the opportunity to empower their representatives to that government. Escalating tensions reached even as far as New Mexico and resulted in stoppage of Santa Fe trade.

A few months after Lincoln declared a state of insurrection and called for volunteers, soldiers stationed at western forts headed east to answer the call; and Confederate troops from Texas, marching over eight hundred men into the territory, quickly took advantage of New Mexico's depleted army ranks. Commander of the Confederate Army in the Southwest, Brigadier General H.H. Sibley, soon joined those forces, and the Confederates successfully took both Albuquerque and Santa Fe.

New Mexican officials set up a temporary capitol in Las Vegas's Exchange Hotel built in the previous decade by Santa Fe traders. But volunteers swiftly combined with Colorado's troops, and, fifteen miles east of Santa Fe at Glorieta Pass, they fought victoriously, sending the Confederate Army back to Texas. The "Gettysburg of the southwest" ended potential Confederate extension into New Mexico and Colorado.

Then, with Confederates having given up and many Union forts abandoned, Indians once again felt a misleading glimmer of hope for surcease of traffic into their territory, hope that was destined to become tragedy. As the United States met the challenge of divisive civil war, the new southwestern population, usually without supervision from Washington, addressed its Indian problem. While seven hundred thousand men responded to President Lincoln's call for volunteers, while brothers, cousins, and friends fought each other at Shiloh, Bull Run, and Fredericksburg, General James Carleton assumed military command of New Mexico. Determined to "exterminate" the Indians and clear the land of what he considered to be a major obstacle, he epitomized America's prevalent attitude toward its native-born population.

Tribe after tribe faced the last throes of their fight against the white man's invasion. Paralleling the Union's ravagement of the Confederacy, General Carleton began his own war against Apaches and Navajos. With construction of Fort Sumner, one hundred fifty miles south of Cimarron near the Bosque Redondo, the "Star Chief" planned a so-called home for the Indians, a place where he could convert savages into Americans. Even before provision for quarters or food had been implemented, he sent four hundred Mescalero Apaches to the Bosque Redondo.

Carleton remained in charge of New Mexico's military installations until well after the Civil War ended, leaving behind him and his "bluecoats" an Indian population that had little alternative but hatred for Americans. When President Lincoln issued the Emancipation Proclamation in January 1863, General Carleton was preparing instructions for the ultimate campaign against the Navajos; and in the following June, Lucien's friend Kit Carson, now a colonel in the United States Army, received orders to advance with force against the enemy.

By the time Sherman had completed his devastating march through the south, with a blazing climax in Atlanta and triumphant arrival in Savannah, eight thousand Navajo Indians had marched, defeated and starving, over four hundred miles to Carleton's Bosque Redondo on the Pecos River. There they joined their enemies, the Mescalero Apaches, to barely exist for more than four years in a prison-like encampment that promised only shortages of food and limited supply of water. Carson, who had volunteered to serve in the Union Army and had followed his superior's orders to completely subdue the Indians, reported for duty at Bosque Redondo as acting superintendent over the seven thousand individuals he had defeated.

In the southwest, while the Union gained victories at Gettysburg, Vicksburg, and Chattanooga, yet another group of Indians fought in renewed anger against the white men. But, after two years of fighting Carleton's soldiers, seventy-two-year-old Chiricahua chief Mangas Colorado, taller than most men both in stature and reputation, entered the white soldiers' camp under a flag of truce, seeking peace. Imprisoned and murdered, his body was left in the dust, its head removed, later to be sold to an eastern phrenologist.[9] Following Mangas Colorado's death, Cochise and Victorio assumed command, leading the Chiricahua in bloody yet hopeless outrage against the white invaders.

Even as isolated as New Mexico's northeastern corner was, Lucien Maxwell felt repercussions of the war between the states. The Indian Agency for Southern Utes and Jicarilla Apaches was transferred from Taos to Cimarron, his ranch becoming their headquarters and meeting place. Remaining tribes of Utes eventually agreed to treaties, in 1863 and 1868, that defined reservations and surrendered most of the one hundred fifty thousand square miles claimed by the "Blue Sky People." Relationships with all American Indians suffered from Washington's inattention and a lack of connection between authority and any reliance upon that authority. Only after gold or silver was discovered did anyone get interested in making the new territories part of the United States.

In the absence of any other form of government, Lucien Maxwell's influence and authority expanded. His agricultural operations profited because of increased need for supplies at Fort Union, site of the quartermaster for the Army of the Southwest, and Cimarron prospered. However, as death permeated the rest of the country, even Cimarron's powerful master could not avoid meeting it face to face. A series of personal losses followed the all-too-brief interlude of peaceful family life that had begun with his daughter Verenisa's birth.

Shortly after the bloodiest day of the Civil War, when almost five thousand men were killed at Antietam, Lucien's mother died in Kaskaskia, sixty-nine years old. On November 11, Lucien wrote to his uncle in Illinois:

> *Should my mother when she died have owed or is indebted to any person please advise me of the amount and I will remit it to you on the receipt of your letter as I do not wish any of her personal property sold. As you said in your letter it was my mother's wish that Sophie should have all of the personal property my mother's last wish is mine so far as I have anything to say about the matter. By attending to this you will confere[sic] a great favor on your nephew*
>
> *LBM*[10]

Meanwhile, as the year 1864 passed, they fell, one by one, relatives and friends. First, in February, at the age of sixty-four, Lucien's father-in-law, Carlos Beaubien, died. March brought the digging of Verenisa's grave, six months and twenty days after her third birthday. The little girl had comforted her mother and grandmother after the grandfather's death. Within a few months Grandmother Pabla herself died, only fifty-three years old, having grieved so, the family said, over the loss of her grandchild that life was no longer worth living. Pabla Beaubien's youngest child Pablo, Luz's brother, was only sixteen years old, same age as Luz's son Peter. Surely Lucien Maxwell was reminded of the time when he was a boy of fifteen, losing siblings and father. Thirty years had gone by and, at the age of forty-five, he must have felt the closeness of death's specter-like presence.

In that spring when Verenisa died, Navajo Indians defeated at Carleton's orders began their funereal "Long Walk" to the Bosque Redondo. In late fall, shortly after observance of America's second official Thanksgiving holiday, Colonel John Chivington led an attack at Sand Creek against Black Kettle and his tribe of peace-seeking Cheyennes. The chief stood confidently under two flags, a stars and stripes given him some years before by an American officer and a white flag of truce;

but Chivington and his men prevailed with an unmitigated hatred of Indians. Word of the unnecessary and deliberate violence against women and children of a peaceful enemy echoed across the nation. Colonel Chivington had "deliberately planned and executed a foul and dastardly massacre which would have disgraced the veriest [sic] savage among those who were the victims of his cruelty."[11]

Everything that was happening around Lucien Maxwell pointed in one direction, that being his own mortality. He clearly saw himself approaching the age his father had been when cholera had struck, years earlier back in Kaskaskia. He saw his two oldest children, Pete and Virginia, the same age he had been. He saw Luz and the little ones she would be left with in the event of his death. He must have realized the time had come to consolidate his assets and provide for his family's future.

Within only a few months he paid three of Luz's four sisters for their shares of the grant, inherited under Carlos Beaubien's will: three thousand five hundred dollars to Theodora and her husband, the same amount to Juana and her husband, and three thousand dollars to Eleanor and her husband. As for the remainder of Beaubien's lands, Luz's father, prior to his death, had offered to sell his interest in the million-acre Sangre de Cristo Grant to William Gilpin. Gilpin, whom Lucien knew from the Frémont expeditions of twenty years earlier, had been appointed governor of the Colorado Territory, and he already owned a share of the grant. Beaubien's estate honored his offer to Gilpin, concluding the sale for fifteen thousand dollars, and Lucien also sold his one-sixth interest to the eager purchaser for six thousand dollars.[12] In that way he probably acquired sufficient cash to obtain the sisters' interests in the lands where he and Luz had established their residency.

At that time the land office showed no significant sales in New Mexico, and there is no evidence leading to the belief that Lucien Maxwell planned on selling out. He seemed to be merely tightening his ownership of the grant. After all, three years passed before he and Luz bought the fourth sister's interest. When, in February 1867, Maxwell paid Luz's sister Petra and her husband, Jesús Abreú, three thousand five hundred dollars for their inherited share of the Beaubien lands, according to Abreú, "there was no market" for land at the time and it was of no particular value.[13] Not until the decade's final months did Lucien purchase Luz's young brother's portion. Pablo, who was only sixteen when his father died, returned to Cimarron to live with Lucien and Luz after completing his education at the Vincentian school in Sainte Genevieve.

One last chunk of money was required to accomplish total and complete ownership of the Beaubien and Miranda Grant, and with this final acquisition Lucien gained his first view of what might lay ahead. Shortly before his forty-eighth birthday, the District court approved an eighteen thousand dollar settlement of a lawsuit initiated many years prior to Beaubien's death.

Legal action claiming one-third interest in the grant had been brought by the heirs of Charles Bent, the governor who had been killed in the Taos massacre of 1846. Charles was to have received the land in exchange for work toward establishing a colony but died before he could accomplish his part of the bargain.[14] The court's decision in favor of the governor's heirs, though for one-fourth rather than one-third of the grant, pushed Lucien to settle prior to the court's actual division of the land. His payment of six thousand dollars to each of Charles' three children in exchange for their legal interest satisfied the court.

Legal convolution, however, had only just begun. Since Bent's son Alfred had died before the lawsuit reached the courts, his share went to his widow on behalf of their two children. The widow's new husband claimed she had not been paid and pressed on with further legal action. Lucien, enraged, supposedly responded, "I'll law 'em until hell freezes over and then law them a day or two on the ice."[15]

A quarter of a century after Lucien's death, the Supreme Court of the Territory of New Mexico eventually decided in his favor, ruling that there was no evidence of fraud. Legal problems arising from the Bent heirs' claim, however, dwarf in comparison to what followed Lucien's sale and departure from Cimarron. That morass enveloped all occupants and claimants, legitimate and otherwise, until the end of the century.

Having experienced this first lawsuit, Lucien Maxwell could not help but know that the future held more of the same, and, at first, he was prepared to take on all comers. He had but a short time left to enjoy his Cimarron country before the world found out about the gold that lay underneath its soil. During those years business was good. Maxwell's three-story-high mill gathered Utes and Jicarilla Apaches for weekly flour rations; its gear-driven grinding stones filled three hundred sacks of flour daily.[16] The towering stone walls rose like a monument a few hundred yards west of Maxwell's house, destined to stand in the next century as the last remaining physical remnant of his Cimarron enterprises. The mill's completion in November 1864 marked the turning in destiny's plans for Lucien Maxwell.

The United States, too, reached a turning point the following April when John Wilkes Booth's assassination of President Abraham Lincoln permanently inked the calendar in black, only a few days after General Lee's surrender at Appomattox Court House. Over a million men had been wounded or killed in the Civil War, more than a third of its participating soldiers. So much blood was shed that in Tennessee a clear forest pond at Shiloh turned red.

Though President Andrew Johnson attempted to implement Lincoln's plans for reconciliation between North and South, radical Republicans demanded retribution against a rebellious Confederacy, causing a bitter takeover of an already destroyed South. With most former leaders disenfranchised, "carpetbaggers" intent on reaping profit for themselves assumed leadership of newly elected state legislatures. It was a time of "easy pickings" in burned cities and previously productive but now desolate farms. Northern urban population had found wealth in wartime production, but veterans returning to the south found no hope. Some, having seen vast lands available in the west, moved away and started over.

Convergence of east and west began. Agricultural Nebraska joined the union as its thirty-seventh state, but, in the east, industrial complexity replaced agrarianism. John D. Rockefeller, not yet thirty years old, established the Standard Oil Works in Cleveland, Ohio; and Andrew Carnegie, who, at thirty, had worked his way up from "a $1.20 a week bobbin boy in a cotton factory" to division manager of the Pennsylvania Railroad, was starting out in the iron business.

Mail service resumed and telegraph communication connected New Mexico with eastern cities. Even fourteen-thousand-foot peaks of the Rocky Mountains could no longer serve as a barrier. Hordes of people were coming a lot closer to New Mexico and they were sure to find the gold that thus far remained unmined.

Years later, it was told that Lucien knew about gold on the grant long before it was discovered. Rancher William Hoehne testified that in 1862 he heard Maxwell tell some miners from Texas that there was gold on his grant and that "the time had not come yet when it could be worked." Arthur Morrison, also under oath, recalled hearing in 1865 and 1866 about gold on the Maxwell grant and distinctly remembered a conversation between its owner and himself. There was, Maxwell told him, "a good deal of gold there and [Maxwell wanted] to buy out some heirs . . . and get the thing in better shape."[17]

Instead of gold, Lucien's attention focused upon harvesting wheat and putting up hay, tending herds of sheep and cattle, supervising timber cutting and construction, and upon stocking and selling merchandise in his three stores. His innovative agricultural methods and introduction of new breeds to New Mexican livestock benefitted the entire territory with lasting influence. Cross-breeding Cotswold sheep from Vermont with the fine wool-producing Spanish Merino increased his herds to twenty-five to thirty thousand. Likewise, in his cattle operation, importing short-horned bulls resulted in better beef for tastier steaks, which were in great demand back east. He invested thousands of dollars, not only in animals but also in equipment, bringing in machinery otherwise unaffordable to northern New Mexico's farmers. Lucien wanted to make his land top-quality and as productive as possible. Every animal he owned, even dogs and chickens, were "of the same style—the best that can be had."[18] Employing hundreds of men in his multiple operations and receiving a percentage of annual crops from farmers on the grant, Lucien became a very wealthy man.

To outside observers all was going well in the landowner's life; but, following shortly after the decade's midyear, something changed. In October 1866, Indian Superintendent A.B.Norton wrote his superiors recommending purchase of the Maxwell Grant's "one million six hundred thousand acres" for a reservation, noting its availability at a price of two hundred fifty thousand dollars.[19] What went on in Lucien Maxwell's mind will never be known. But the change in direction can not be disregarded, and close in time was the discovery of gold.

As the story goes, soldiers from Fort Union recognized copper among some rocks traded with Indians from Maxwell's. When they went to investigate on Baldy Mountain's western slope, the men found gold in Willow Creek. The following spring Lucien and the discoverers formed the Copper Mining Company, immediately filing a claim. By summer the word had spread, and what had been could be no more.

A year later, when Marcus Brunswick and John Dodd approached him about investing in the Big Ditch, a water project that was to facilitate placer extraction of gold, Lucien Maxwell told Dodd, "I am tired of this place from the Indians and the newcomers on the land, and I will sell you the whole grant, everything I've got." Dodd thought the price Mac asked—two hundred thousand dollars—was more than he had and more than the property was worth."[20]

It seems more than coincidental that Indian affairs at that time had reached an all time low. Navajos imprisoned at Bosque Redondo faced failure of corn crops, and, with wartime complications of hauling supplies overland, their lives remained in the hands of General Carleton. The small fertile oasis on the Pecos River could support a few hundred individuals, but sustaining the nine thousand who were confined there was beyond its most exaggerated capabilities, even under favorable conditions. Crop failures all over the territory followed during the next year, which was the worst any man then living could remember. "No part of New Mexico enjoyed immunity from disaster. Heavy frosts nipped the buds and blossoms, and destroyed the fruit from one end of New Mexico to the other. Torrential hail and rain storms at one time, and devastating drouths at another, seemingly conspired to thwart man's efforts to produce the fruits of the earth. Locusts and grasshoppers descended on fields of wheat, corn, and beans in the granary counties of Taos, Mora, Rio Arriba, and San Miguel, devouring every stalk, branch, and blossom. Crops of every kind were a total failure."[21]

Not only Navajos faced desperate conditions. The United States government reneged on its promise under terms of its 1863 treaty with the Tabeguache Utes to deliver livestock and goods for ten years. With early snow thwarting their annual buffalo hunt, the tribe faced winter without provisions.[22] At the Cimarron Agency, Utes and Apaches "were in a pitiable condition, hungry and nearly naked."[23] And Ute Chief Kaniatche, with whom Kit Carson and Lucien Maxwell had experienced a special understanding and relationship, now grieved and angered over the death of his son, went on the warpath.

In the next year, Luz's brother, eighteen-year-old Pablo Beaubien, returning home from school, was attacked by Indians on the Santa Fe

Trail.[24] Though he survived, Lucien and Luz must have been reminded of the loss of her other brother and all the memories of the terrible scene at Taos twenty years earlier.

Finally, General Carleton's military command of New Mexico came to an end, largely as a result of strenuous opposition on the part of Doctor Michael Steck, Superintendent of Indian Affairs for New Mexico, and his successor, A.B. Norton.[25] Norton's memo to his superiors, dated October 1867, reiterated his earlier recommendation to purchase the Maxwell Grant for two hundred fifty thousand dollars and complained that his previous report had been completely disregarded.[26] Repeated efforts to obtain suitable lands for an Indian reservation met with repeated disregard. Lucien Maxwell began to seek other buyers.

Change was inevitable; but during the last years of the 1860s, in a place where money was scarce, satisfactory exchange of goods more than likely permitted all connected with Maxwell to live better than they might have elsewhere. Those who benefitted included Indians who had been purchased from capturing tribes, Lucien's adopted daughter being one of those. Deluvina believed that her adopted father had bought her for ten horses from Apaches who had stolen her away from the Navajo people. She lived to be quite old, remaining loyal to Luz and the family, and later recalled that Navajos, Utes, and Apaches often visited "Tata Makey." Always upon their arrival, she said, he directed that a cow be butchered, and he himself supervised its preparation. Then, at his invitation, the Indians helped themselves to the feast.[27]

Lucien Maxwell was "Tata Makey" or "Father" to many of the fifteen hundred Indians who lived on the grant and had earned a reputation of one who trades in good faith.[28] He was their friend and shared their lives. One visitor wrote of finding Lucien "seated on the steps of his house in shirt sleeves, surrounded by a motley group of squaws, papooses, and warriors, painted up and decorated in their usual style. They had just ridden in from the mountains on a visit . . . and all seemed on the most familiar terms with him — talking and laughing while the children played around."[29]

Extending hospitality to anyone and everyone, Lucien evidently savored his ability to afford better than average living conditions. The Cimarron house had been designed in three sections, one for family, one for visitors, and one for servants. Ornamental furnishings decorated some rooms while others had only a table and chairs for the men who entertained themselves playing cards. In the rectangular main room, empty except for a few tables and chairs and his desk, Lucien "received his friends, transacted business with his vassals, and held high carnival at times." Henry Inman described his stays at Cimarron:

> I have slept on its hardwood floor, rolled up in my blanket, with the mighty men of the Ute nation lying heads and points all around me, as close as they could possibly crowd, after a day's fatiguing hunt in the mountains. I have sat there in the long winter evenings, when the great room was lighted only by the cheerful blaze of the crackling logs roaring up the huge throats of its two fireplaces built diagonally across opposite corners, watching Maxwell, Kit Carson, and half a dozen chiefs silently interchange ideas in the wonderful sign language, until the glimmer of Aurora announced the advent of another day. Not a sound had been uttered during the protracted hours, save an occasional grunt of satisfaction on the part of the Indians, or when we white men exchanged a sentence.[30]

Men who had risked everything in earlier years amused themselves by betting on poker hands. Lucien, a serious gambler, meticulously collected at the end of an evening every cent he had won, but he was known often to lend funds to a heavy loser the very next morning.[31]

Horse racing, too, provided excellent opportunity for gambling, Lucien betting one or more of his rapidly growing collection of highly bred animals against all comers and even going so far as to build a race track near his house."[32] Hiring Squire Thomas Hart to care for his horses, Lucien allocated large amounts of money to raising, breeding, and gambling. He employed jockeys to race for high stakes, but he himself rode all over the grant's lands in every sort of vehicle, from the plainest buckboard to the colorful, rocking Concord coach. For a man who had survived the mountain snowstorms and waterless deserts, risking an accident while traveling over his own land was a small thing. "He was perfectly reckless in his driving, dashing through streams, over irrigating ditches, stones, and stumps like a veritable Jehu, regardless of the consequences, as is usually the fortune of such precipitate horsemen, rarely coming to grief."[33]

But, even as he was acquiring great wealth, Lucien Maxwell, as he approached his forty-ninth birthday, could hardly have avoided the turmoil and disruption that lay ahead. The Indians might have perceived an unusual accident that happened about that time as an omen. Lucien and a captain of the troops stationed at Cimarron were injured while shooting a rusted old cannon. The soldier's injury necessitated the surgeon's emergency travel from Fort Union to the ranch, where he provided life-saving treatment to the captain and bandaged Lucien's seemingly insignificant wound. When, after a few days, the landowner's thumb did not heal and amputation was required, Inman and Carson rode with their friend in his coach to the doctor's Fort Union quarters. Colonel Inman wrote of the evening's surgery:

> *Maxwell declined the anaesthetic prepared for him, and sitting in a common office chair put out his hand, while Carson and myself stood on opposite sides, each holding an ordinary kerosene lamp. In a few seconds the operation was concluded, and after the silver-wire ligatures were twisted in their places, I offered Maxwell, who had not as yet permitted a single sigh to escape his lips, half a tumblerful of whisky; but before I had fairly put it to his mouth, he fell over, having fainted dead away, while great beads of perspiration stood on his forehead, indicative of the pain he had suffered.*[34]

In spite of such difficulties, Cimarron's boss was, by year's end, fully involved in mining. Just as he had collected rents from farmers in the form of produce, Lucien charged for placer mining, a process that required water to separate gold from gravel that lay in stream bottoms. For underground mines, he demanded half ownership and, in exchange, handled any dispute with claim jumpers.[35] Any wealth he had acquired earlier dwindled in proportion to what his new assets were about to produce. Miners and merchants moved in quickly, more than four hundred people living in Cimarron and nearby communities, mainly Elizabethtown. At first, supplies and food were hauled fifteen miles up the road from Lucien's ranch along the Cimarron Canyon, mule-driven wagons crossing the river thirty-three times. Within a year, a toll road constructed by the grant's owner permitted Concord coaches to travel the twenty-six miles to Elizabethtown in six hours; by then, over two thousand people resided in the new town.[36]

In addition to forming his own company to work numerous mines, opening stores that sold necessary supplies and food, building roads, and running his immense agricultural operations, Lucien made plans for a company to construct and operate a forty-mile ditch that could provide water for placer mining. Sales of small acreages to various individuals interested in Santa Fe Trail traffic brought more incoming cash. One such purchaser, Uncle Dick Wootton, promptly constructed a toll road across Raton Pass, which of course was free to its former owner.

Lucien Maxwell, at the apex of his business life, did enjoy the fruits of his labor. Henry Inman's description, though it glorified and romanticized, remains one of the few firsthand accounts of how Lucien handled his money:

> Maxwell was rarely . . . without a large amount of money in his possession. He had no safe, however, his only place of temporary deposit . . . being the bottom drawer of the old bureau in the large room to which I have referred, which was the most antiquated concern of common pine imaginable. There were only two other drawers in this old-fashioned piece of furniture, and neither of them possessed a lock. The third, or lower, the one that contained the money, did, but it was absolutely worthless, being of the cheapest pattern and affording not the slightest security; besides, the drawers above it could be pulled out, exposing the treasure immediately beneath. . . . I have frequently seen as much as thirty thousand dollars - gold, silver, greenbacks, and government checks – at one time in that novel depository. Occasionally these large sums remained there for several days, yet there was never any extra precaution taken to prevent its abstraction; doors were always open and the room free of access to every one, as usual.
>
> I once suggested to Maxwell the propriety of pur-

chasing a safe . . . , but he only smiled, while a strange, reso-
lute look flashed from his dark eyes, as he said: "God help the
man who attempted to rob me and I knew him!"[37]

His successful entrepreneurship as merchant and trader seem
to be in direct conflict with a reputed absence of concern over accounts
due him, but his seemingly careless handling of money was offset by
the distinct impression that he was in control of his "empire." Attorney
Melvin Mills later condescendingly recalled, Lucien "never wanted to
do business in a business way, but preferred to take another's word,
and never wanted to write anything down."[38] But a hotelkeeper who
lived on the grant said the custom at the time was to trust "to the honor
of each other."[39] Over and over, plaintiff's witnesses in the *Bent v. Miranda*
lawsuit used identical words about Maxwell's relationship with Indians and Mexicans: "total control," "could make them do anything he
wanted them to," "a very resolute man," "willful." Yet, under cross-
examination, they admitted that he maintained that control "some probably by fear, and some by kindness."[40]

The grant's diverse population had different opinions of its
owner's character but certain consistencies emerge from their varied
descriptions. Squire Hart who cared for Maxwell's horses over a six-
year period commented, "He was a very resolute man. That was his
reputation. . . . I don't think it was safe for a man to oppose him. . . . If
any person had attempted to jump any portion of this grant he would
have either run him off or killed him."[41]

A banker from Trinidad said, "He was a man that was resolute,
a little bit arbitrary, but I don't hardly think he was willful."[42] Calvin
Jones, who had a quarrel with Lucien Maxwell and "quit him" at the
time of the sheep drive to California, then later worked for him again,
said,

His power was just as if he owned the whole outfit, the same
as a man who owned slaves in the south before the war. . . . If
a Mexican servant didn't suit him or did anything against
his orders he took a board or plank or anything he could get
hold of, and whipped him with it. . . . He generally ran his
own court. A couple of men broke into his storeroom one night

and took almost two hundred dollars worth of goods . . . started
south . . . when the horse gave out, one [going] to Rayado and
one back to house. . . . [When they found] the man who had
the goods there peddling, they brought him back to Cimarron.
Maxwell took a big log chain weighing about forty pounds
and a padlock and locked it around his neck . . . locked him to
a block down in the cellar . . . forty-six hours.

Jones claimed that Lucien "had no regard to the law of the land" and also told of the time he "took his sixshooter and shot it off" at a constable who came to Rayado after Indian George."[43] Yet Lucien's granddaughter remembered his carrying no weapon, only a small pocket knife."[44]

The society in which they lived was, for all intents and purposes, lawless, yet Maxwell demanded and received either respect or fear from all with whom he dealt. Had money been the end-all of his ambition, accounts would have been kept to the letter. The fact that they were not, and that he was able to live in the manner of *ricos,* is in itself an acknowledgement of his adept leadership.

Jacob Beard, who traveled to California with Maxwell, testified, "his word or his paper was good for any amount as long as I knew him. . . . I never saw the man in all my life that wielded as much influence over the community; people of all classes . . . . There was no limit to his courage that ever I saw."[45]

William Walker, stone mason and soldier stationed at Fort Union during the war, knew Lucien Maxwell's "generosity, hospitality, and disposition to do what was right by everybody and to treat everybody right. . . ." Walker noted that Indians and Whites alike respected Lucien and Mexican and American families who worked as shareowners on his land depended on him for their livelihood. "If they paid for it, it was all well and good, and if they did not it was all well and good anyhow. The Mexican people, both men, women and children, and even the Indians, called him father."[46]

Lucien carried out the family tradition. His attitude toward other people, as well as his house with its covered porch extending across the width of the adobe structure, greatly resembled that of his grandfather Menard. Teachings of Saint Vincent, learned so many years earlier at

Saint Mary's of the Barrens, continued to influence his daily living. And that daily living continued to revolve around his land.

Lucien was known to express sincere concern for observant Penitentes who lived on his ranch. These men observed extreme rites of penance during Holy Week, imitating their Savior's punishment during the last week of his life, re-enacting the march to Calvary and the crucifixion. Lucien Maxwell sent food on Holy Saturday to break their fast and salves for wounds inflicted during the ritual performances. For such help and understanding he earned their gratitude. According to historian William Keleher, "When spring merged into summer, nothing pleased Lucien B. Maxwell more than to walk barefooted on his lands and dip his feet in the cooling waters of an acquecia in the alfalfa fields, and discuss with his Penitente friends topics relating to field and farm. . . ."[47]

Accounts of his generosity were recorded during sworn testimony of even the prosecution's witnesses at the *Bent v. Miranda* trial:

I have seen as high as fifty people set down to his table and partake of his hospitality. Nothing was ever charged by him for meals or feed for their horses. In fact his house was the resort of old timers, and people from afar and near army officers and others. I myself was in the service part of the time and stationed at Fort Union, and knew of my own knowledge that the government availed themselves of his services on several occasions to keep quiet among the Indians and settlers his influence was so great. . . .

He was a man that nothing in the world would prevent him from accomplishing what he undertook to do. I inferred that partly through respect that every one had for the man, and partly from his determined character, no one ever undertook to stand between him and any object that he might have in view, and not that he ever undertook to bulldoze anyone but that he had a peculiar way of winning everyone over to him, without any brow-beating.[48]

By the decade's latter years, many other sites along the trail offered resting places for travelers, but only Lucien Maxwell is remembered and recalled with such clarity. Other men erected homes which were, by New Mexico standards, mansions and the equal of his "palace" in Cimarron. Samuel Watrous, same age as Lucien Maxwell, planted thousands of trees around his twenty-five room home in La Junta. Fourteen fireplaces heated the u-shaped dwelling, its fine furnishings brought by wagons along the Santa Fe Trail: "the beautiful vose piano, boxes of books with fine leather bindings, the heavy carved Victorian furniture of mahogany and walnut, the marble-topped tables and dressers, the gilt-framed mirrors and gilded clocks, the hand-painted lamps and fine china dinner service."[49]

Don Vicente Romero's productive fields and effective irrigation system, along with a three-story mill, made his ranch an important source of supplies for nearby Fort Union. His stately home, with its polished wooden floors and windows set deeply in the two-foot-thick adobe walls, became the center of a sizeable settlement on the Mora River. Twenty-two room "La Cueva" boasted two stories and a ninety-foot, two-story porch.[50]

José Albino de Baca, owner of a mercantile business and much of the land around Las Vegas, built a three-story house for his fourteen-year-old bride. Eighty-six and a half feet wide by ninety-eight feet long, the third floor's wooden walls and shingled roof topped lower floors made of lime-plastered, white adobe. The ground level of a two-story veranda was paved with flagstones.[51]

Whatever was unique about Lucien Maxwell's hospitality made his place known in all the territory. Most individuals who testified against Maxwell during the Bent trial had stayed at his home, eaten at his table, and rested in the shadow of his protection. He established himself, according to one newspaper, as "one of the kindest, most generous and charitable men that lives."[52]

As profits poured in, purchases of furniture and decorations for his home aroused considerable admiration, and undoubtedly some envy, from all visitors. Later, very few ever bothered to recall leaner days of Lucien's younger years, only the extravagance after gold became part of his life. The daughter of William Morley, manager of the grant during its English ownership, wrote about Cimarron, describing her childhood wanderings through the house, her awe of its four pianos and Victorian-style furnishings: "Room after room had its deep-piled carpets, heavy velvet draperies, [and] gold-framed oil paintings."[53] How much of this grandeur was added by new owners after his sale and subsequent departure from Cimarron cannot be reliably determined. This is the present memory amply fed by legend.

In reverse proportion, as Lucien's wealth increased, his control of the grant's vast acreage decreased. Some evidence points to the possibility that he expanded the boundaries of the grant to include gold-producing areas, but it is also possible that boundaries were never important until squatters and claim jumpers began arriving. He did begin securing leases from miners and collecting rent. No longer could a handshake and a man's word suffice. Also important to note is the fact that it was not until immediately prior to sale of the grant in April 1869, long after Lucien's purchase of Miranda's share of the grant, that he required Pablo Miranda to execute a quitclaim deed to officially formalize his father's sale.

Lucien, throughout the decade, continued with bold investments. Incorporating the Moreno Water and Mining Company, he prepared to go ahead with the "Big Ditch" project, an amazing idea for its time. His personal investment of one hundred fifteen thousand dollars, majority of the company's capitalization, suggests his never-flagging willingness to risk. He wasted no time in putting up capital for another promising project, becoming a five-twelfths owner of Baldy Mountain's Aztec mine and immediately sending an ore sample to the government assayer in Denver. When the first quartz sample indicated a yield of close to twenty thousand dollars per ton in gold, the partners hired Colonel E.H. Bergmann to take charge of the operation. Freighting in equipment and engines from the nearest railroad station on the other side of Raton Pass, they commenced serious operation. "A twelve horsepower stationary steam engine propelled batteries of fifteen stamps weighing four hundred twenty-five pounds each so that they dropped at the rate of thirty-three times per minute." In seventy-one days of operation between November and April, the stamps crushed eight hundred fifty tons of rock and produced almost thirty-seven thousand dollars.[54]

Even as Lucien Maxwell advanced through months preceding his fiftieth birthday, claiming every opportunity to enlarge his fortune, he could not overlook the cost that far exceeded his monetary investment. As news spread about gold on the Maxwell Grant, as it was now called, potential speculators came, and squatters established mining sites without paying rent. Soon the once relatively obscure lands chosen so carefully by Beaubien glittered with unmined gold. Atchison, Topeka, and Santa Fe Railroad engines raced to replace the Santa Fe Trail's wagon caravans.

Not only was the old symbol of commerce between two cultures fading but so was everything that accompanied its passage through unknown territory. It was too late to stem the tide of change that was rising against the Cimarron country. It had been too late even on July 5, 1865, when Senator Doolittle opened his investigation of Indian Affairs in New Mexico and Colorado. Too late when Carson and William Bent helped forge the Medicine Lodge Treaty that set up reservations for Cheyennes, Kiowas, Apaches, and Comanches. And too late when dying Kit Carson traveled to Washington, D.C. and met with the President and Ute chiefs who reluctantly agreed to a reservation on the eastern one third of what became the state of Colorado. Also too late when Secretary of War Ulysses S. Grant directed the project at Bosque Redondo be abandoned.

As western buffalo herds and Indians steadily decreased in number, impeachment efforts proceeded against President Johnson, unsuccessful by only one vote, reconciliation of North and South foundering; and passage of the fourteenth amendment to the Constitution defined citizenship, including Negroes born in the United States — but not Indians.

In June, five years after their impoundment at Bosque Redondo and two years after Carleton had been relieved of his military command in New Mexico, Navajo Indians began their month-long journey homeward. Only three weeks earlier, the man who had accomplished their defeat died. Kit Carson and Lucien Maxwell may have seen each other for the last time when Carson, after release from the military, traveled from Santa Fe to his home at Boggsville near the Arkansas River. One of the few assets revealed upon probate of Carson's will was a three thousand dollar note signed by Lucien Maxwell.[55]

In August, Lucien's brother Ferdinand, older than Lucien by six years, suffered a stroke, aftereffects of which confined him to a wheel chair for the duration of his life. Also during that year, Luz's sister died, thus leaving both Luz and Lucien again affected by loss and sickness in their respective families. In November, Custer attacked Cheyennes on the Washita River; and this time Chief Black Kettle, who had spoken for peace, who had been brave enough to attend treaty talks, and who had somehow survived Sand Creek four years earlier, was killed.[56]

By Christmas, on what would have been his friend Kit Carson's fifty-ninth birthday, the Utes met for a conference at Cimarron. At the time four groups of speculators were talking with him about purchasing his land, and he knew that St. Vrain, in Mora, was also being approached.[57] Lucien Maxwell understood that grants securing New Mexico's northeastern corner would be sold by owning families, and he moved closer and closer to a decision.

Everything in Cimarron had changed, the town now lying within newly created Colfax County. Early in the year following his fiftieth birthday, the community he had built elected Lucien to the official position of Colfax County Probate Court Judge by an overwhelming margin of more than three hundred votes.[58]

By the last year of the decade, there were twelve to fifteen thousand Anglos in the New Mexico Territory among a total population of over ninety thousand. Native New Mexicans moved eastward across the Canadian River, and new communities dotted the high plains. Then, as New Mexicans were spreading eastward, Texans expanded westward, stretching their cattle industry to the same grassy openness. Cowboys began moving herds northward to meet the railroad that transported cattle to Chicago's Union Stockyards.[59] There, meatpackers Armour and Swift paid thirty or forty dollars a head.

Forty-five-year-old John Chisum, whose immense herds numbered well over fifty thousand, moved into the Pecos River Valley. Charles Goodnight and Oliver Loving, driving thousands of cattle to market, opened a trail northward to Colorado, and, in the process, got to know Lucien Maxwell.

Goodnight took as partial payment for a herd a ten-thousand-dollar note signed by Lucien Maxwell to a freighter who had delivered goods to the Cimarron store. Lucien had been able to pay only small amounts toward the entire debt; but, after gold was discovered on his land, he advised Goodnight that, though he didn't have sufficient currency, "he could pay off in solid gold at the mine." From a hollow log Don Luciano, as he was called by his Mexican tenants, took out several chunks of gold, each one "the size of a guinea egg . . . enough [Lucien said] to set a hen." Goodnight, admittedly far from knowledgeable about the value of gold, found when he returned to Texas that Lucien had overpaid him by about a hundred dollars.[60]

Lucien was becoming richer and richer. The Aztec Mine alone, from October 1868 to December 1869, yielded almost nine thousand ounces of gold valued at one hundred seventy-five thousand dollars.[61] By spring, the owner of the mine had made up his mind to sell. The years of transition from Old West to New West ended abruptly.

As the final tie in the transcontinental railroad was hammered into place at Ogden, Utah, on May 10, 1869, the old man of the Santa Fe Trail, William Bent, traveled over Raton Pass one last time, perhaps stopping at Cimarron before heading north. On May 19, less than a week before his sixtieth birthday, William Bent died.

On May 26, Lucien and Luz Maxwell signed an option for sale of the Beaubien and Miranda Grant, at a purchase price of six hundred thousand dollars. They didn't yet own the last share that Carlos Beaubien had willed to his children. Papers for Luz's brother Pablo's portion were not signed until the first day of the following year, for an amount similar to what other members of the family had received: three thousand five hundred dollars. A few weeks later, the wagon carrying Kit and Josepha Carson's bodies to reburial sites in Taos passed by Lucien's house. The old trail and the stops along its path were coming to an end.

By the end of the 1860s the United States of America had farther extended its physical boundaries with purchase of Alaska from Russia for seven million two hundred thousand dollars; and the maturing nation's population equalled that of France and Britain, with New York and Philadelphia having attained ranking as major cities of the world. The Suez Canal opened and efforts to initiate a canal in Panama were under way. The nation in 1870 was buying a half million sewing machines a year, and E. Butterick and Co's pattern plant in Brooklyn was sending out more than six million patterns a year.[62]

Ulysses S. Grant, only forty-seven years old when he took office as eighteenth president of the United States, gave radical Republicans a free hand to reconstruct the south as they saw fit; and the next several years turned out to be one of the most corrupt times in the history of the country with everyone seeking power. Angry southern men dressed in white sheets protested, and eastern speculators fought over whether the government should redeem its greenbacks in gold. In September, ten days after Lucien's fifty-first birthday, Jim Fisk and Jay Gould tried to corner the gold market but President Grant ordered the sale of four million dollars of government gold. The price plunged and many speculators were ruined on what became known as Black Friday.

In New Mexico, as the decade ended, two young men who had graduated in the class of 1860 from the University of Missouri, Territorial Attorney General Thomas Benton Catron and United States District Attorney for New Mexico Stephen Benton Elkins, opened law offices. Their eventual partnership impacted New Mexican economics and politics until the end of the century through a circle of power eventually to be known as the Santa Fe Ring, a circle which widened in circumference in direct proportion to lengthening future legal battles over the Maxwell Land Grant.[63]

There, at the edge of the Sangre de Cristo Mountains, aspen gold gave way to autumn, and a cold wind preceded Thanksgiving Day, seventh since President Lincoln had first declared the national holiday. On Christmas Day a meteor streaked across New Mexico's sky. The Reverend Thomas Harwood, Methodist minister newly assigned to the New Mexico Territory, was on his way to Elizabethtown. He wrote in his journal, "It looked as large as the moon right in daylight. It was almost as bright as the sun. It seemed so near, I wondered why I did not hear it strike the earth."[64] Lucien Maxwell, seeing the unusual brightness, must have thought back to that November, over thirty years earlier, when stars had streaked across Kaskaskia's skies. He had traveled so far, accomplished so much, and yet, he was preparing to start all over again. But he was, after all, a New Mexican now, and the Land of Enchantment would surely show him the way.

6

FORT SUMNER ON THE PECOS
1870 TO 1875

The United States of America stretched from Atlantic to Pacific with railroads, electric lights, and open hearth steel furnaces. Urban centers on the eastern seaboard and vast lands west of the Mississippi River offered unlimited opportunities. Rising plains and soaring mountains offered fulfillment for children of immigrants who wanted a piece of the earth to call their own.

Lucien Maxwell had preceded the onslaught by twenty years, working during those years to build his Cimarron country. On January 1, 1870, Luz's brother, Pablo Beaubien, age twenty-one, signed final papers transferring his inherited interest in the Beaubien and Miranda Grant to his sister and her husband in exchange for three thousand five hundred dollars. It was the last step in their acquisition of over one million seven hundred thousand acres of land in the United States Territory of New Mexico. More than the land, there was the thriving town where he and his family lived, where a three-story mill centered the populace in their efforts to make a living for themselves; there was Elizabethtown and Baldy Town; there were copper mines and gold mines, the Aztec alone producing forty-eight thousand dollars a year; there were sawmills at Ute Creek and Elizabethtown that yielded over twenty-five thousand dollars annually;[1] there were herds of sheep and cattle and a stable of horses; all this in addition to their home!

During the years of Lucien's empire-building, as his brother-in-law Abreú confirmed, no one was interested in paying for land. Lucien's ability to accumulate enough funds to put together that empire reveals both determination and farsightedness. His father-in-law's activities further validated what Lucien had learned from his father and grandfather, that the most desirable asset was land owned free and clear. With the discovery of gold and other minerals in Colorado and New Mexico, the growing cattle industry, and new railroad lines, interest in southwestern land grants attracted all kinds of attention.

On January 28, 1870, Lucien and Luz accepted ten thousand dollars for a revised option from Jerome Chaffee, Charles Holly, and George Chilcott. The Maxwells agreed to sell their land and all improvements for one million three hundred and fifty thousand dollars, everything with the exception of the thousand acres that was their home ranch, some parcels already sold to specified individuals, and the Maxwell interest in the Montezuma and Aztec mines. Lucien was fifty-one years old and Luz, in her early forties. Within nine months he would reach his fifty-second birthday. Everything in their lives would be different: family, business, and home. Some of the changes he was prepared for, had planned for; others just happened, completely and totally unexpected. Having made up his mind to sell, and being the man of action that he was, Lucien probably accepted the lengthy process as a necessity to be tolerated, any emotional upheaval already dealt with; but with the arrival of spring he faced something he had not anticipated. Oldest daughter Virginia, only recently having returned from Saint Louis where she had completed her schooling, departed from their Cimarron home. Secretly married on March 30 to Lieutenant A.S.B. Keyes, who had been assigned to the Cimarron Indian Agency a few months earlier, Virginia sent word to her father of their marriage as she and her husband left for Lieutenant Keyes' next assignment.

Much has been written and surmised about Lucien's supposedly violent reaction to the news; but he was not unaware of their feelings for each other, a Denver newspaper having earlier made mention of Keyes' affection for Maxwell's daughter.[2] According to the Methodist minister who married the young couple without her parents' knowledge or consent, nineteen-year-old Miss Maxwell had a mind of her own and was determined not to wed the man of her father's choice.[3]

Lucien, in the midst of accomplishing his sale, also had to accept the fact that his daughter was not going to be at his side in whatever future operations he had planned. But whatever his anger or disappointment at the time, there was no lasting rift between them; and, in spite of suggestions that such may not have been the case, Virginia remained a Catholic as did all future generations of her family.[4] All evidence points to the probability that Lucien and Luz enjoyed the presence of grandchildren during their last years together.

Within days of his daughter's departure with Lieutenant Keyes, Lucien Maxwell, on April 30, signed a deed relinquishing title to almost two million acres of land. Two weeks later the Secretary of the Territory approved Articles of Incorporation for the Maxwell Land Grant and Railway Corporation and authorized capital stock in the amount of five million dollars. Since ownership by foreigners might complicate the sale, three prominent New Mexicans officially represented the English syndicate: William A. Pile, governor of the Territory; Thomas Rush Spencer, surveyor general of the Territory; and John S. Watts, chief justice of the Supreme Court of New Mexico.[5]

To receive the money due him, closing arrangements had to be made with the English purchasers; so Lucien traveled to New York City where he spent several weeks awaiting transactions that would release funds directly to him. The eastern metropolis abounded in activity. Horse races on Long Island surely attracted his attention and perhaps, tired of his city confinement, Maxwell rode some friend's horse in Central Park. Maybe he saw the White Stocking Baseball Club of Chicago in its twenty-sixth appearance defeated by the New York Atlantics. Or perhaps he rode one of the two steam-powered elevators to the seventh floor of Manhattan's "skyscraper." Even if he didn't visit, he heard about J. Pierpont Morgan's house, the first New York residence to be lighted with electricity.

He was in New York City on the Fourth of July to watch fireworks and parades. Bells in Trinity Church's old steeple rang out in both an early morning and mid-day serenade. On Wednesday, two days after celebration of the nation's ninety-fourth birthday, Lucien Maxwell placed a final signature on the deed. A man accustomed to being surrounded by vast spaces, he walked the few blocks between the law firm on Williams Street and the New York Stock Exchange, more than ready to return home.

Only the witnessed signature of Luz Beaubien Maxwell was required to complete the sale, that to be done as soon as the purchaser transferred the specified amount to Lucien. His friend Marcus

Brunswick, who had accompanied him to New York City, returned to New Mexico and left papers with Luz. Finally, Lucien telegraphed Cimarron, "New Mexico all right." And Luz's signature completed the transaction. The buyers paid less than one dollar an acre; the sellers received about six hundred thousand dollars. The real estate sales team of Chaffee, Chilcott, and Holly apparently retained their fee, and the purchasers assigned their rights to the Maxwell Land Grant and Railway Company. Lucien Maxwell supposedly asked for fifty thousand dollars in cash, much of which he promptly spent for gifts to take home.[6]

No longer the owner of two million acres of land in New Mexico, he departed eastern shores and made his way westward, at least part of the way by train, and surely remembering the first time he had crossed the vast lands between Kaskaskia and the Rocky Mountains. Lucien's granddaughter related the story of an event that supposedly happened during the last part of his journey back to Cimarron. "On the way down from Trinidad with a driver of the hack, he camped near where Raton is now." Supposedly two "mean looking men" told the driver that they "knew Mr. Maxwell had the money, but that they didn't care to try to get it." The next day those same men robbed the Overland Stage of twenty thousand dollars.[7]

A rising momentum carried the former landowner into what would be the final five years of his life. On July 23 the sale was recorded in Colfax County record books. Within six weeks Lucien Maxwell sold for an additional one hundred twenty-five thousand dollars the Cimarron house and all of the remainder of his Colfax County property.[8] On September 14 he celebrated his fifty-second birthday, and a few weeks afterward purchased property at Fort Sumner, two hundred miles south of Cimarron.

Autumn nights grew colder and leaves disappeared from aspen forests that only one month earlier looked like melting gold pouring down the mountain sides. In October the caravan departed Cimarron, Luz and Lucien with their family and two hundred or so others.[9] The building that had been Fort Sumner's old officers' quarters was to be their new home. Along with their son Pete and Luz's brother Pablo, both twenty-two years old, were daughters Emilia, age eighteen, either soon-to-be or already married; Sofia, age sixteen; Paulita, six; and Odile, only little more than a year old.

Why? Why did he leave his Cimarron country? Lucien Maxwell was a millionaire at a time when the word had only recently been added to the country's vocabulary. His departure not only puzzled his descendants but also has fascinated historians and storytellers well into the present time. A variety of theories reflects a like variety of opinions but it is in the consistencies of character that the answer lies.

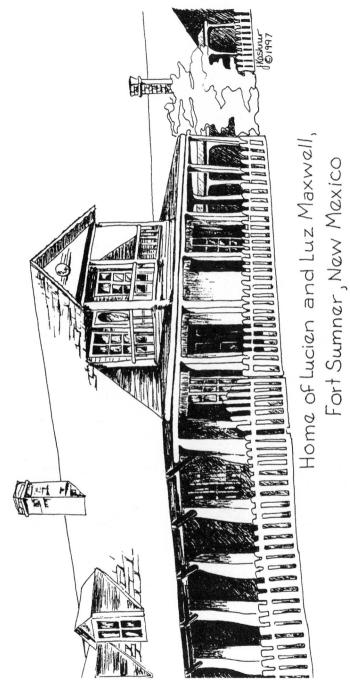

Home of Lucien and Luz Maxwell,
Fort Sumner, New Mexico

JKoskinar ©1997

Was he, as some contemporaries claimed, an opportunist who, from the beginning of his life in Taos, saw the grant as a money-making scheme, marrying Beaubien's daughter to secure his own interest, building and acquiring over twenty years, then enlarging the original acreage into a gigantic land steal?

Or was he a builder, giver rather than taker, who knew for years the immensity of the acreage described in the original grant and, likewise, the existence of gold, which he began to dig out only after it was discovered by the outside world?

Some naysayers suggest that Lucien Maxwell was literally taken for a ride, hoodwinked, outsmarted, by men who were far worldlier than he; that young Elkins and his law partner Catron used the older man to benefit their own ends and left him by the wayside once they had accomplished those ends. Others suggest that his health was already failing, that his zest for living had ended, that his business ventures had failed, that he was suffering financially.

A likely scenario must include Lucien's knowledge of the growing interest in northeastern New Mexico's unsettled lands and his astute awareness of the endless legal tangle of claims and counter claims that were going to be a part of those lands. Not only speculators from eastern urban centers but also moneyed Europeans eyed with a degree of awe the vast resources under land grant auspices.

"In the two years prior to 1870, there were only ten original homestead entries filed, and in that year there were ninety-six."[10] Suddenly, settlers sought lands under the Homestead Act; miners scrambled for what was underneath the land; railroad tycoons wanted transportation fees in addition to accompanying lands granted by the federal government. Everyone brought the American way, never heeding the New Mexican life-style essential to the individual who wanted to survive in a land that was so different from whence he had come. Maxwell had used the old ways, changing, adapting, blending, all to make his land productive; but, with the influx of outsiders who knew only their own way of land division, native Mexicans were forced to recognize arbitrary metes and bounds. Their accustomed pattern of owning small sections extending outward from waterways was no longer acceptable, and communal land holdings, a principle of many original grants, became a thing of the past. Eventually, in most cases, easterners' failure to understand and take into consideration such differences brought ultimate failure to their attempts to subdue the land. They apparently wanted only to take, never to become part of and build.

Prior to the discovery of gold, interest from the outside had been nil. People of Cimarron, their leader included, lived their lives according to rules they themselves created. Those who came to be farmers and sheepherders knew and accepted conditions of frontier life, more than likely welcoming orderliness in the community which Lucien established. Don Luciano was their *patron* and represented their interests. As settlers, they wanted to work the land and raise families there along the river at the foot of the mountains, occupy a few acres without question and without excessive rents. Their *patron* claimed a portion of produce and crops for which he provided a market where exchange and trade provided, in turn, desirable goods otherwise unavailable. As their leader in the enterprise of settlement, he exacted a profit based on their profit along with respect for the rules he made.

At a time when theft was expected and even accepted, no one stole from Lucien Maxwell. People prospered under his leadership and his reputation protected them. Lucien Maxwell had built his home and brought his family, added furniture and machinery and jobs. For as long as he could, he held the land and people of the grant together. When he left, he tried to move on to a new area of productivity.

For Lucien Maxwell, the year 1870 climaxed five years of increasing conflict with impending changes and, more than likely, an accompanying sense of his own mortality. A man who had always prided himself on self-sufficiency and his ability to get along was no longer young at fifty-one years of age. His father had died at age forty-three. Best friend Kit Carson died at age fifty-eight. Health problems may have already begun to appear, causing him to doubt his own physical ability to care for not only himself, but his family and all the many other people who depended upon him for subsistence and survival.

Luz was still relatively young at forty-two and, as a widow, with parents gone and the youngest of their six children only a year old, unprovided for, would be forced to remarry. True, she had her brother-in-law and sister at Rayado and her twenty-one year old brother Pablo who had completed his schooling, but Luz, even with the help of her family, was not going to be able to withstand the legal battles required to retain title. Lucien Maxwell knew only too well about land grants and title validation, as well as effects of escalating property tax, and he knew, too, the world would not overlook New Mexico much longer.

The decade brought momentous changes, not only for Lucien Maxwell, but for the entire country. With total United States population approaching forty million, California passed the half million mark, and the Rocky Mountain area exceeded three hundred thousand. While New Mexico remained at one hundred thousand, change had already reached the Colorado Territory on the other side of Raton Pass. Denver's wealth centered Colorado's two hundred thousand people.[11] And William Palmer bought land at the base of Pike's Peak for what was to become present day Colorado Springs and the Denver Rio Grande Railroad.

National expansion headed in a southwesterly direction, perhaps in hopes of leaving behind populations and politics east of the Mississippi where north and south remained separated, where southerners, economically and culturally destitute, felt abandoned by their country. Newly freed slaves, guaranteed rights by fourteenth and fifteenth amendments to the United States Constitution, were left unassisted and directionless by Yankee politicians.

While Lucien and his family were departing from Cimarron, Robert E. Lee died, on October 12, 1870, never having been granted a full pardon by relentless "conquerors," and the other well-known Civil War general now resided in the White House. Lucien Maxwell had lived through eleven presidents' leadership. For the first time, his country's president was younger than he was. This president and most of the eastern population viewed the west in a new light, no longer land belonging to Indian nations but rather their own path to wealth and a place for popular amusement.

Lucien's fifty-second birthday marked endings and beginnings. Older, wealthier and maybe even a little wiser, experienced risk-taker, successful rancher, farmer, and entrepreneur, known throughout New Mexican Territory, he had paid his dues. It had cost more than gold, of which he now had plenty.

He and Luz had shared a quarter of a century, twenty-five years having passed since he had been with Frémont at Utah's Great Salt Lake. There, on his twenty-seventh birthday, he and Carson had ascended Pilot Peak in search of a stream to which they could lead the fifty-some others in Frémont's expedition. By Christmas of that year he had journeyed across the Great Basin and the high Sierras, and it was the next Christmas before he returned home to Taos and his young bride.

In those earlier years money had not been readily available; but he had managed to come up with cash to purchase Miranda's share of the grant, and, following his father-in-law's death, the interests of Luz's sisters. He had paid what the courts said the Bent heirs were due. He had built a home for his family and welcomed all, as his grandfather had done before him. Though he entertained his guests in ways considered luxurious for that place, personal aggrandizement claimed little of his attention. His horses, contemporaries said, received more attention than his wardrobe.

According to a young lawyer who was not an admirer, Lucien Maxwell "was a heavy set gruff sort of a man, who dressed in the most slouchy way, and always wanted to cuss somebody when things did not go his way." Melvin Mills remembered his early employer: "No one knew when he might turn loose on them, hence many people avoided him. . . . He was very loose in his habits, he gambled, drank whiskey, though he never got beastly drunk, and I think it would have taken a barrel of whiskey to get him very drunk. He would sometimes favor an Indian in preference to a white man."[12]

By New Mexico standards Lucien had lived a life of ease. His children had been educated at Catholic schools and his wife had servants to lighten her responsibilities. Lucien, to either the extreme like or dislike of those around him, had his own way of doing things, a way that resulted in profit. With cattle herds that numbered in the tens of thousands and at least twelve thousand acres under cultivation, revenues continued to increase.[13]

Gradually, an ever-increasing presence of insincerity, false admiration, and malicious envy replaced friendship and laughter. As more and more people learned of Lucien Maxwell's "mansion" and his gold, increasing numbers of uninvited intruders invaded his lands, begrudging him his way of life and seeking to pursue their own interests at his expense. Profiteers climbed over the mountains, taking from the land without care or concern for anything or anybody.

Interlopers and squatters took land, but life took parts of the man. One by one his cohorts from the early days departed. Joe Doyle, who some thought was the richest man in the Colorado territory, had died at the age of forty-six, and his widow shortly afterward, their wealth quickly disappearing as the object of fortune-hunters.[14] Then, in October, shortly after the Maxwells' departure from Cimarron, a huge crowd gathered at Mora for the funeral rites of William Bent's former partner, Ceran St. Vrain.

Death came to the Indians with whom Lucien had traded and yes, fought and killed, but also had lived side by side with. Since 1861, when the Indian Agency was moved from Taos east of the Sangre de Cristos, Jicarilla Apaches and Utes had gathered in Cimarron. Efforts to sell his land to the government for purposes of an Indian reservation had failed. Lucien could not have avoided a sense of failure as he witnessed the government's abandonment of responsibility.

He had overcome many difficulties for many years, sustained injuries, scrambled through seemingly untraversible mountain passes; but all semblance of balance on the grant met an oncoming tide of people who cared nothing for the land or its previous possessors, White or Indian. Gold, that was what they were interested in; not trade, not fairness, not honesty. Takers, they took advantage of "boom time" and planned to stay no longer than was necessary to extract the minerals; transients, they had no desire to make the land produce, to trade on their labors, and could produce only an immediate locust-like excision of the earth.

Some optimism remained, however. Even before leaving Cimarron, Lucien Maxwell entered a new venture. Congress had authorized federal charters for privately-owned banks along with a national currency secured by government bonds. Putting up one hundred fifty thousand dollars, the former landowner funded the First National Bank of Santa Fe. It was the first commercial bank in New Mexico and in 1995 celebrated its one hundred twenty-fifth year of operation, the only one of seven banks chartered in Santa Fe before the twenties of this century to have survived. Lucien had served as unofficial banker in Cimarron for years, handling money when cash was at a premium, his reliable desk drawer always containing gold and whatever was necessary for his community to function. Such was the role of most frontier merchants, who also were obligated to fund local horse races as entertainment, "prepare and finance the Fourth of July celebration; pay for the music at the Indian dances when he visited their villages near by, and interest himself in the welfare of his customers of whatever grade."[15]

Lucien assumed the presidency of the new bank, had stock certificates printed with his picture, and designated a formal seal, a wild Indian surrounded by the words, The First National Bank. Of course he retained a large amount of the stock, one thousand two hundred seventy of the fourteen hundred shares issued. Intentionally and completely overlooking the others who had accomplished the sale of the grant, he made Charles Holly, son Peter, Judge John Watts of Cimarron, and Henry Hooper officers and principal stockholders.[16]

After the initial September meeting in Cimarron, there was some delay in obtaining the currency required to open the bank. Holly traveled to New York in December, attempting to expedite granting of the charter. Finally, in February, one hundred thirty-five thousand dollars in small bills arrived in Santa Fe by army ambulance and with a soldiers' escort. In mid-April the bank opened for business.

By the following month, however, Lucien was out of banking. His partners Elkins and Catron evidently disagreeing with whatever he was doing, pulled away, obtaining a charter for a second bank, and exerting some sort of pressure upon the former landowner. When the stockholders met again on May 17, Elkins, Catron, and Griffin were officers and majority owners. Some say Lucien and his "Cimarron Crowd" were bested by the "Santa Fe Ring," but, interestingly, a rather unusual loan was made by the bank at exactly this time, in the amount of forty-five thousand dollars, to its former president, Lucien Maxwell. Also to be noted from the bank statement of July 14, 1871, is the absence of what must have been Lucien's significant holdings following sale of the grant. He had several hundred thousand dollars but his account was not at the First National Bank. It seems then that he simply withdrew his funds and left, finding it not worth the effort to be involved in banking. Such a conclusion seems consistent with his evident separation from all he had earlier owned and operated.

Maxwell's timing proved perfect, freeing him to go on with his life. Five thousand dollars purchased the buildings at Fort Sumner, which had been deserted two years earlier by the United States Government following departure of the Navajo from Bosque Redondo. Though completely unsatisfactory and inadequate for thousands of Indians, the former military installation provided a place quite ample for Lucien, his family, and a small community of ranchers and farmers.

Completely different from Cimarron, where high treeless plains abutted forested mountains, Fort Sumner's settlement offered a view both east and west, both sunrise and sunset visible across the horizon. Two rows of cottonwood trees extended four miles northward from the fort's buildings; visible remains of Indian crops and beginnings of a dam marked its landscape; and, at the site of the Maxwells' home, the river valley's greenness widened to almost three miles. Though in summertime the water was said to be brackish, or sour to the taste, it provided ample moisture for the dense growth of black grama, one of the most nutritious grasses for livestock. Reliable winter range and grass that cured on the ground stood ready to receive grazing cattle and sheep.[17]

Among the twenty-five or thirty families who accompanied the Maxwells from Cimarron to Fort Sumner was Lucien's old *caporal*, Jesús Silva, who was to supervise the ranching operation at the new location. Within a very short time nine thousand head of cattle, some from the former lands of the grant and others from stock purchased around Fort Sumner, required Silva's full attention while Maxwell himself oversaw agricultural interests. In addition to cattle and horses, a sizeable sheep herd later reached seventeen thousand in number under the charge of daughter Emilia's husband, Manuel Abreú.[18]

Some of the Spanish-American families built small adobe houses and farmed the forty acres of irrigated land assigned as their own. Others lived in various buildings that had been part of the prior operation of the fort. Luz, Lucien, and the children resided in some fifteen to twenty spacious rooms of the remodeled officers' quarters, resuming their life without the intrusion of gold seekers.

Twenty years earlier Luz had traveled across the Sangre de Cristos with her two babies, joining her husband at Rayado. Now, she and Lucien, no longer young, were beginning again, but this time with considerable wealth and loving family around them. The land was different and not even their own.[19] The graves of their dead lay far away; but roots gained ground along the Pecos; and families continued to grow. Before the year's end Berenice Mary was born there at Fort Sumner, Lieutenant and Virginia Keyes' first child starting another generation, father and daughter reconciled after his anger at her secret marriage.[20]

Three more of Virginia's children were born before her father's death, young Maxwell spending most of his first five years with grandparents at Fort Sumner.[21]

As Virginia had told the minister who had performed the ceremony, "My father is not a vindictive man."[22] And Lieutenant Keyes proved to be an individual worthy of Lucien's daughter's affections. From a family that included participants in the American Revolution and a governor of Massachusetts, he continued in the military tradition, promoted to captain's rank within three years of their marriage. Grandchildren Berenice Mary, Alexander Hugh, Maxwell, and Lucy Beatrice must have delighted Luz and Lucien, easing their passage into the older generation. Daughters Odile and Paulita had to have looked upon the babies as sisters and brothers rather than nieces and nephews.

At a crossroad of the southwest, railroads, cattle, and trade developed quickly on the Pecos River; and increasing activity called for individuals like Lucien Maxwell, men who excelled at supplying goods to markets desirous of exchanging other goods, men who could act decisively without undue fear of what lay ahead, men who followed cattle trails to places so far away that mail delivery required sixty days.[23]

A hundred miles north of Fort Sumner and already a major trading center, the town of Las Vegas, where Major Kearny had first made his proclamation to New Mexico of United States takeover, boasted a population of two thousand.[24] Its location on the still busy Santa Fe Trail attracted "cattlemen, sheepmen, soldiers, miners, prospectors — they all needed supplies and Las Vegas . . . was where most went to get them. . . . [It] took on a cosmopolitan atmosphere as increasing numbers of foreign-born immigrants settled in the town alongside the Hispanic pioneers."[25]

Lucien Maxwell was only one of the visitors who came to town for amusement. He had always liked playing cards and was known to be a participant at gambling tables. The hotel in Las Vegas was a "popular meeting place for all the cattle barons from southern Colorado and northern New Mexico, and all such occasions were signalized by a big poker game . . . the ceiling alone being the limit."[26]

Gambling amused the aging Maxwell and his race horses were widely known. From Fort Sumner he issued a "Challenge to the World" that ran in the *Santa Fe Post*:

*I will run my mare " Fly" against any mare, stud or gelding
in the world, four hundred yards, for from five to forty thousand dollars, to carry catch weight on each.*

*If any person will accept this challenge for twenty
thousand dollars, I will allow him one thousand dollars for
traveling expenses: or if they will accept it for thirty thousand dollars or upwards I will allow two thousand dollars for
expenses. The race to be run at Las Vegas, New Mexico. This
challenge to be open for three months from this date.*[27]

At least one taker resulted and Ben Dowell's mare, Kit, bested
Fly. A second horse of Maxwell's beat Dowell's stallion Ned. "An estimated twenty-five thousand dollars in bets changed hands."[28]

Grandchildren and horses were not the only things in Lucien's
life at this time. At Fort Sumner, where the cattle industry was on an
upswing, his success in raising superior beef was already recognized.
His background in Illinois, where the industry had matured years earlier, stood him in good stead. Like Chicago, where critical access to transportation connected small farmers with large markets to become a pri-
mary receiving area for the nation's livestock, the Maxwell settlement
in Fort Sumner provided all necessary ingredients for a major marketing center. With its river location along the main cattle trail and as the
site of a licensed trading post for twenty years, Fort Sumner proved to
be an ideal place to connect the cattle industry with increasing demand
from eastern markets through midwestern packing companies.

By the time Lucien moved to Fort Sumner, trade along the
Goodnight Loving Trail was well established, and the amount of money
handled by its western bankers was enormous. In 1871, seven hundred
thousand cattle arrived in Kansas where banks in Kansas City handled
three million dollars in cattle money and in Omaha, a half million.[29]

Lucien already knew Charles Goodnight. And he also knew John
Chisum, "Cattle King of America" and his nearest neighbor on the Pecos
River. With a herd estimated by various sources at between fifty and
seventy-five thousand, Chisum eventually settled fifty miles south of
Fort Sumner, running his cattle over some hundred fifty miles along the
Pecos River. As his neighbor Lucien Maxwell had done before him,

Chisum sold out, his herd in 1875 worth several hundred thousand dollars.[30] Unlike Maxwell, however, Chisum, a few years afterward, departed New Mexico. Both men had envisioned enormous potential in lands on the Pecos River banks, where nutritious native grass provided ample feed for livestock that could supply extraordinary demand from eager Eastern and European buyers, and when mechanical improvements in meat handling and refrigerator cars facilitated transport to a widening market.

Everything pointed to a strengthening beef industry but its results were not entirely beneficial. While railroads transported cattle eastward to stockyards and slaughter on the other side of the Mississippi, they also carried destruction in a westerly direction. Easterners who wanted no part of the hard work of building towns and communities saw great adventure in travel across the prairie, in observation of "wild" Indians and buffalo. In 1872, the Atchison, Topeka, and Santa Fe Railroad brought tourists to Dodge City, Kansas, where men amused themselves by shooting at buffalo from train windows, and the firm of Wright and Rath handled as many as eighty thousand hides at one time.[31] In 1873, eight hundred tons of meat and a quarter of a million hides from slaughtered buffalo were shipped from western Kansas.[32]

Grassy plains that had fed the buffalo became open range for the thriving cattle industry, and a new image brightened the imagination as cowboys brought herds of cattle into railroad shipping points. Then, as iron rails extended westward, farmers and ranchers settled around them, sometimes paying up to ten dollars an acre for lands granted to owning railroad companies by the federal government. Alternate sections, retained by the government for public sale, were to be offered at two dollars and fifty cents per acre, but that could only occur once construction was completed, usually several years later. Subsidized in this manner, railroads dominated America's financial scene, attracting large and small investors and speculators. Their advertising inundated newspaper pages of eastern cities and towns, luring farmers to land that supposedly could be made profitable and productive with a little hard work.[33]

Lucien, in the year following the move to Fort Sumner, demonstrated forward thinking with a contract, according to the *Daily New Mexican*, to build one hundred fifty miles of track on the Texas portion of the Southern Pacific line for forty thousand dollars a mile .[34] Railroads, he must have realized, could connect Fort Sumner and southern New Mexico with markets east of the Mississippi as well as California. Until 1875, rail connections into Texas didn't exist. "The only way to get into Texas, except by foot or horsepower, was by rail to New Orleans, then by steamer to Galveston and then by rail to Houston." All necessary materials for construction of railroads, including rail cars and locomotives, had to be sailed in on schooners, a very expensive undertaking.[35]

Said to have been not so successful was Lucien's supposed investment of two hundred fifty thousand dollars in railroad bonds, but no reliable information authenticates the story. He knew speculation had proven to be the ruin of many would-be railroad tycoons. One acknowledged failure, the unbuilt Memphis and El Paso Railroad, had been backed by none other than his old leader, John Frémont, chartered prior to the Civil War and planned to include a western line between San Diego and Fort Yuma, Arizona. The possibility exists that, just prior to the failure of the railroad enterprise, Lucien, while in New York City, may even have visited Frémont at his home in what was then a fashionable part of New York City between Fifth and Sixth Avenue on west Nineteenth Street.[36]

While western towns thrived, several financial problems arose in eastern cities. An immense fire swept through Chicago's business district, resulting in property damage of two hundred million dollars. Then, within a few days of Lucien Maxwell's fifty-fifth birthday, the bank that was backing a second transcontinental railroad failed, setting off a financial panic and subsequently a nationwide depression that saw more than a million people unemployed. At the same time, yellow fever hit the Mississippi Valley; drought denuded the Great Plains; and swarms of locusts stripped the prairie of everything green.

Economic difficulties in the rest of the country made Lucien Maxwell's cash assets extremely beneficial. While Lucien was enlarging his Fort Sumner operation, playing poker, and racing his favorite horses, the rest of the country began hearing about the grant that bore his name and the mountains of gold that had made him a millionaire. At fifty-five, Lucien Maxwell was already considered old, the tough years having claimed their price. Most of what people say about him today describes his last few years at Cimarron, a life that seemed to easterners like another world. Newspaper clippings, stories, and descriptions all dwell upon horse-racing and gambling; a novel presented a fictionalized account of the "Baron." Quickly forgotten were his early struggles,[37] when merely surviving required expertise far beyond the average individual's capability. Lucien lived only five years after leaving the Cimarron country, and many individuals have suggested, without proof of any kind, that he was near bankruptcy at the end of his life. Those detractors fail to take into account what it meant to have an impressive amount of cash during the 1870s. In addition to what he received from sale of the grant, his copper and gold mines had already yielded fortunes. Investments during the last ten years of his life indicate, even at his advancing age, Lucien's characteristic willingness to take a risk. Some ideas worked; others didn't.

Neither in assets nor in attitude could Lucien Maxwell's last years be considered a failure. Rather, his life mirrored the transition that was going on all around him. Technology, war, and the monetary system pushed people together, each affecting the other more directly. Previously separate, compartmentalized parts of the country were forcibly brought into contact with each other. The Santa Fe Trail, which had begun as a commercial roadway, gradually changed to a passageway for people who were interested in merely getting from one part of the country to the other. The federal government broadened its protective energy over its western people and their industries. In exchange for that protection, westerners agreed to live under its laws. Lucien Maxwell had lived his life, making decisions, willing to bear the consequences of his decisions, and gradually accepting that government's presence in his life, both as military protector and validator of his ownership of over one million seven hundred thousand acres of land.

Young Lucien's childhood home had prided itself on its history and envisioned a future that recaptured its past glory, a future that did not rely upon the protection of a larger government entity, but rather upon the townspeople themselves. Above the bar in Kaskaskia's single hotel hung a painting of an imaginary city, a plan for the future, detailed with churches, a variety of public buildings, and public squares.[37] Lucien, too, had a plan for his own future. He had built in a place where there had been only the land and the people. When that place could no longer be what he envisioned, he left. He was not a failure but times had changed.

While Lucien Maxwell began again two hundred miles to the south, his former domain reeled in the repercussions of those changes. The former owner had not been insistent about clarification of title and had worked out agreements with descendants of the families who had lived on the grant prior to his own cultivation of its lands. Farmers paid for their land by applying annual production toward a reasonable price and by paying nominal rents. Most miners paid, either in rent or in shares of ownership of their lodes. Contrary to such precedent, the Maxwell Land Grant and Railway Company pressed hard, meeting resistance from all sides. "Following the sale of the Grant, Maxwell turned over his account book containing the produce paid by various settlers with the understanding that the agreements would be honored. The Englishmen did respect the rights of those listed, even though deeds had not been issued to them. But they were also determined to assert their own rights. Polite notices were first sent to all families warning them either to make suitable arrangements with the company or vacate its holdings. When it became apparent that most nontitled settlers were not willing to relinquish their homes, farms or ranches without a struggle, ejectment proceedings were inaugurated."[38]

Not surprisingly, at the departure of Lucien Maxwell and his family and followers from Cimarron, violence and disorder erupted. It didn't take long for everything to "bust loose." Almost immediately an uprising broke out in Elizabethtown, protesting against company agents who attempted to enforce eviction notices; and in April of the following spring, an angry mob seized control of company property.[39] The fight against the "foreigners" continued until the final decision of the Supreme Court of the United States in 1887 made further war futile.

In addition to complications in claiming title, financial problems plagued the Maxwell Land Grant and Railway Company. Speculators who had purchased Lucien's land hoped to change the Santa Fe Trail into a railroad bonanza and mother lode of gold. The English purchasers of the grant incorporated a New Mexico Company and immediately placed a first mortgage on their newly acquired property in the amount of seven hundred thousand pounds sterling, about three and a half million dollars, and utilized a Dutch company to handle bond sales. Within two years of the original purchase, the company placed a second mort-gage against the property in the amount of two hundred seventy-five thousand pounds sterling. Clearly, selling bonds for a quick profit re-ceived far more attention than running a successful agricultural opera-tion. Advertisement and promotion of the land and its resources offset income from bond purchasers, and the company was weighed down with long-term liability, obligated to pay yearly interest of nearly three hundred fifty thousand dollars.[40] It could not last long.

With the old owner gone and the new owners busy making their fortunes, one problem magnified, overshadowing the Maxwell Land Grant and Railway Company's two million acres. The problem had arisen early in the process of Lucien Maxwell's sale and it would not be finally settled until many years after his death.

Lucien knew, when once he made up his mind to sell, that a survey was essential to making it happen. When New Mexico Surveyor General T.Rush Spencer reported to the United States Commissioner of the General Land Office that Maxwell had made a deposit for and was beginning a survey of his land, the grant's dimensions were called into question. Old Mexican law limited governors' grants to eleven square leagues, or about forty-seven thousand acres, a very small portion of lands within the description of Beaubien and Miranda's original pa-pers. Secretary of the Interior Jacob Cox studied the matter. On Decem-ber 31, 1869, Secretary of the Interior Jacob Cox decided that Beaubien and Miranda were entitled to only eleven leagues each, that the claim of over four hundred fifty leagues was not valid. The original survey was called to a halt and William Griffin, the same Griffin who became the only paid employee of the First National Bank of New Mexico, was re-hired, on an unofficial basis, to complete the survey, his employment being "entirely unofficial and extralegal."[41]

Completely ignoring the decision of the Secretary of the Inte-rior, option holders Watts and Chaffee proceeded to pursue sale of Lucien's land. The position taken by Lucien Maxwell and his advisors rested upon Congressional recognition and approval of June 21, 1860, following Beaubien's initial filing for patent. But questions over valid-ity of the company's title gave fuel to unhappy settlers who refused to recognize the Maxwell Land Grant and Railway Company's right to collect payment from them.

Charges of fraud eventually found Chaffee, Chilcott, and Holly, alleging enlargement of the grant's acreage to far more land than supposedly was intended by the Mexican grantor, but the allegations did not hold up in court. A final decision on the grant itself was not rendered until 1887 when the United States Supreme Court refused all appeals and fully recognized the official 1877 survey and subsequent patent of 1879. This confirmed Maxwell's count of the total acres as correct and concurred that the completed survey followed the perimeter described in the grant.

Eventually the Supreme Court's decision rested on congressional recognition and never addressed the earlier limitation. Of the forty-two original Armijo grants recorded with the United States for land in New Mexico and Colorado, thirteen were patented. Only two of those, the Beaubien and Miranda, and the Sangre de Cristo, were acknowledged to contain acreage that exceeded eleven square leagues.[42]

Sellers of the Maxwell Land Grant may have only bordered on legality, but evidence weighs heavily that Lucien Maxwell knew well the size of the lands he claimed and had known, just as Beaubien had, of that size from the beginning. Whether or not the United States was entitled to recognize such grants could possibly be called to question but the intent of grantor and grantee seems clear.

Historian Victor Westphall convincingly argues that, looking at all the grants issued by Armijo, the individual allotments fit together like a "giant jigsaw puzzle," covering the northeast corner of the New Mexico territory as a "buffer" against Yankee invasion. Westphall asserts with considerable evidence, the "mountain men traveled around the area encompassed by it and even passed through some of its choicest areas. They knew its boundaries because they had traveled around them. They knew the geography of northern New Mexico and southern Colorado better than do most modern tourists with road maps. They had to know it because in those days, if one didn't watch where he was going, he damn well got lost."[43]

Lucien, prior to selling, had made no issue of where the boundaries were. It was as far as he could see or ride. That was enough. His earlier actions during the years when he was buying up the Beaubien children's interests reflect self confidence and optimism, even in the face of the lawsuit brought by the Bents. Gradually, though, his optimism deteriorated. Sworn statements of men who appeared to testify in the *Bent v. Miranda* trial, and Norton's letter of 1866, reveal that he was thinking about selling out at least five years before closing the sale, and also that he knew both boundaries and acreage. Reservation at the time of sale for himself and his family of the house and its immediately surrounding acreage in Cimarron indicated caution and his intention to remain there, but the speed with which he changed his mind indicate just how quickly conditions changed. As usual, he did not hesitate but acted upon his decision.

Lucien Maxwell was no babe in the woods. From childhood he had heard his father and grandfather, uncles and cousins discuss land grants. He also had listened to conversations about unsettled and questionable title. Remembering those discussions and the stories he had heard about the difficulties of his Illinois family in claiming lands due them, and having observed with his own eyes the changes gold seekers had wrought upon California and Colorado, Lucien knew well what men would do for gold.

At first, without gold to attract the hordes, New Mexico's land claims had been totally neglected. Although new citizens of the United States were supposedly guaranteed that their property "shall be inviolably respected," the opposite of what was intended under the Treaty of Guadalupe Hidalgo occurred, and only twenty percent of the original Hispanic settlers were able to retain title and use of their land.[44] Eight years passed before Washington finally assigned Surveyor General William Pelham to the New Mexican territory, and, by 1860, over a thousand claims awaited settlement.[45] Until Congress acted on these claims, there could be no "public domain" in New Mexico, and "a paradise for lawyers and politicians had been created."[46]

In an economic environment where barter rather than cash served as exchange for goods and services, land became the usual way to pay legal fees.[47] Attorney Thomas B. Catron, at various times in his life, "owned entirely or had an interest in at least thirty-four land grants . . . [and] represented clients in at least sixty-three land grant cases in New Mexico."[48]

Colorado speculators and British investors purchased one after another of the Mexican and Spanish land grants, the Las Animas in southeastern Colorado, the Sangre de Cristo, the Gervaci Nolan, the Cebolla and Conejos, the Beck, Cucilla [sic], San Cristobal, Cinequilla, Mora, and Los Luceros.[49] Politicians and ambitious men viewed the southwest as the road to riches and power, and gold offered an added attraction to land schemes that benefited originators and agents as opposed to investors and bondholders.

Not unexpectedly, a group formed, a conglomeration of politicians, lawyers, and a variety of other powerful figures of the time, members of both political parties but the majority boasting allegiance to the Republican party. Gathering around Steve Elkins and Thomas Catron after Lucien's departure from Cimarron, the " Santa Fe Ring" produced one principal product, always up for sale: the land.

Early in his process of land acquisition, Lucien sought and became connected with powerful and politically well-situated men. Carlos Beaubien, father-in-law and business partner, and Joab Houghton, were judges of New Mexico's Supreme Court. Houghton later represented Beaubien in initial establishment of title, and Lucien, even later, chose Houghton as his own counselor. Though seemingly uninterested in political advancement for himself, except for his local judgeship, Lucien made certain that he had various politically astute people at his side.

The three men who paid for the option and possibly received the finder's fee — thus accounting for the seven hundred fifty thousand dollars that Lucien did not receive from the sale — were among the best connected in the southwest. Jerome Chaffee, wealthy mine owner and one of the group who chartered Denver's First National Bank, was elected congressional delegate from Colorado in 1870 and would later serve as senator from that state. George Chilcott, who had already served as land registrar for Colorado, was a congressman, and would also serve as senator.[50]

Charles F. Holly, older than his two partners and a contemporary of Lucien's, had been a Colorado legislator prior to his New Mexican residency. He first associated with Lucien shortly after discovery of gold, his expertise as both lawyer and miner proving quite useful. Serving as a principal advisor throughout the sale of the Beaubien and Miranda Grant and afterwards, Holly must have become fairly close to the grant's owner.[51]

Steve Elkins and Thomas Catron also entered into Lucien Maxwell's formidable ranks, but only for a short time, and before they joined as actual partners. Steve Elkins, only twenty-nine when he became owner and second president of the First National Bank of Santa Fe, served as United States district attorney from New Mexico, then as territorial delegate from New Mexico in the United States House of Representatives, and later, for eighteen years, was United States senator from West Virginia. Catron, prior to becoming Elkins' partner, served as United States district attorney for the Third Judicial District and later served as United States senator from New Mexico. "To Palmer, Elkins, Chaffee, and their far-flung associates, the Maxwell Grant—and other grants as well—promised to be a modern Bent's Fort through which the riches of Colorado and the southwest could be filtered, while their railroad would replace the Santa Fe Trail."[52]

A basic difference of values separated Lucien Maxwell from the men who became part of his life in connection with the sale of the grant. He seems to have been well aware that he would need such people to be free and clear of the problems that gold and squatters and title affirmation would bring. Yet he wasted no time breaking connections with Elkins, Catron, and Griffin shortly after their organization of a rival bank. Perhaps he was disillusioned by their obvious lack of loyalty but also, perhaps, he recognized all along what they were. Dealing with them helped him accomplish removal of what had become a burden and he was smart enough to know he could not accomplish in his own way what needed to be done.

Lucien's departure from Cimarron meant giving up a dream, his and his father-in-law's, and that of all the people who had settled there with him, a dream not of gold and riches, but rather of a life in which they could feel rewarded for their hard work. Yet, they did at least have a future to look forward to, unlike the people most affected by sale and departure. Jicarillas and Utes faced a far less optimistic future. President Grant's new peace policy that purported to remove military supervision from America's Indian tribes had little impact on their lives. As control of Indian affairs was transferred from the War Department to the Department of the Interior, their legal status changed from independent nations to what amounted to "wards of the United States government." Congress could decide their fate.[53] Where rivers and mountains had once defined their lands, now surveys and paper maps told them where they could and could not travel. Allure of easy riches pulled white men to the hills without thought of what treaties might or might not allow.

While Lucien hadn't done what William Bent had done twenty years earlier, blowing up and destroying what he had built, he did move away, just leaving it all behind.

When their protector, "Tata Makey," left Utes and Jicarillas to the mercy of the Indian Bureau in northeastern New Mexico, their fate was sealed. They couldn't know that their friend had tried to interest the government in reserving the land for its native occupants. Nor could they understand procedures required for something they had never recognized, documented title and ownership of land. Even so, after Lucien had moved to Fort Sumner, for as long as they were at Cimarron, Utes periodically made the long and difficult journey south to the Pecos to visit their old companion.

Adjustment to overwhelming changes forced both "Tata Makey" and "his" Utes into a different time. With increasing numbers of miners, speculators, and "takers" making their semblance of balance impossible, the former occupants could no longer live side by side among the hills and valleys of the Sangre de Cristos. Like the Santa Fe Trail, the Cimarron country's days rapidly approached an end. True, the land remained the same, Sangre de Cristo Mountains still overlooking the valley, but America had entered what Mark Twain called "the Gilded Age," when corruption permeated the business and government communities. Boss Tweed's manipulations, the Credit Mobilier, and the Whiskey Ring scarred Grant's presidency.

Even in the face of such superficiality, however, indications of America's potentially powerful young adulthood appeared. Elizabeth Cady Stanton and Susan Anthony sought voting rights for women. A young physician named Kellogg managed the Western Health Reform Institute at Battle Creek, Michigan. Fake gold of the Gilded Age failed to affect the people who dealt with real life. There was nothing gilded about Lucien Maxwell. He stood, if only for a brief moment, at a junction of America's history, a symbol of blending cultures and a country's dream.

On July 25, 1875, sixth birthday of his youngest daughter, Odile, Lucien Maxwell died. Only a few days earlier the Feast Day of Saint Vincent de Paul recalled the observance that had marked the end of his school year back at Saint Mary's of the Barrens, so many years before. Don Luciano, as the Mexicans called him; Tata Makey, as the Indians called him; Mac, as his friends called him; the Duke, as Stephen Elkins named him; the man who created Cimarron was gone.

Though some have suggested otherwise, most reliable sources maintain that Lucien Maxwell died of kidney failure, possibly resulting from damages inflicted years earlier. How often had he gone without water, fighting for survival, punishing his body with dehydration that left its ugly scar tissue around kidneys that would finally fail? He surely remembered with unwelcome familiarity the increasing thirst and nausea reminiscent of long days in search of water and, too, his father's body wasting away from cholera's nausea and thirst.

Lucien Maxwell completed half a century of living, having sustained both his friends and his family during at least half of those years. Luz, in her mid-forties with two little ones yet to raise, evidently lived comfortably as a widow. Wisely, she sold her cattle herd before the industry wiped itself out with over-grazing. At age fifty-three she homesteaded a neighboring piece of land, thus starting "new" Fort Sumner.

Louisa Beaubien Barrett, daughter of Luz's younger brother Pablo, wrote about her aunt:

> She was Dona Luz to the Spanish people and to the cowboys she was Mother Maxwell. Always, as they came to town, their habit was to go to the store and deck out. Then they would go to pay their respects to Mother Maxwell, often taking her a gift of some kind. Sometimes it might have just been a pound of cheap mixed candy and sometimes a bottle of Powers Gillispi's best wine. Sometimes they made her real nice gifts. She accepted everything in her own grand way and no matter how poor the present she made the giver feel grand. . . . She was very large and couldn't get around much, but always after dinner she would sit for hours at a time out on the porch in a large chair. There people came to chat with her. The children in the neighborhood and her household were always rewarded. It was this way she disposed of candy and fruit and many other gifts that she was loaded with. Also, she loved to tell us stories about the Indians. She spent many

hours before the little alter she kept in one corner in her room
where she kept a crucifix and an image of the Virgin praying.
She never did any kind of house work, not even to make up a
bed but did bead work and embroidery and pieced quilts.[54]

Luz Beaubien Maxwell lived until July 13, 1900, within two weeks of the twenty-fifth anniversary of Lucien's death, surviving all her children with the exception of Virginia, Paulita, and Odile. She was buried in the military cemetery at Fort Sumner where her husband had been lain to rest a quarter of a century earlier.

Within a year of Lucien's death, the Cimarron Indian Agency was abandoned, leaving four hundred forty-two Apaches who would not be finally settled at the Mescalero Agency in Southern New Mexico until seven more years had passed. The three hundred seven Moache Utes were removed in 1878.[55] Some records indicate that an adopted son, Julian, died of smallpox and was buried at the Fort Sumner cemetery.

On what would have been Lucien Maxwell's fifty-seventh birthday, the murder of Reverend T.J. Tolby exacerbated fighting between "granters" and "anti-granters." Tolby, outspoken in his belief that the grant belonged to the Indians, had decided on a plan to assist the Utes and Apaches and had initiated proceedings for obtaining land along the Vermejo in Colfax County for that purpose.[56]

As a direct result of Tolby's death, another Methodist minister stepped into the fight, Reverend Oscar P. McMains, the man who led "anti-granters" until the final Supreme Court decision. McMains spoke out against his colleague's murder and attempted to investigate. Murder followed murder as Colfax County reverberated with lawlessness. Two weeks after Tolby's death, the man who McMains suspected to be Tolby's murderer, one Cruz Vega, was lynched. "McMains' suspicions enmeshed him in a chain of situations which brought him to trial for murder, caused the sudden death of three men, and precipitated much trouble for the church with which he was affiliated."[57] Granters and anti-granters feuded, physically and verbally, the more recent settlers being among the loudest anti-granters.

What happened to the Beaubien Grant essentially happened to the other grants, but the fact that it was at the beginning of the determination of what was going to happen to the vast lands in New Mexico set it apart as an example for historians. Had the company not carried the name of the grant's previous owner, Lucien's name would not have been sullied. No charges of fraud against Lucien Maxwell were ever proven. Notoriety of the Maxwell Land Grant Company spread as it sought to clarify the rights of squatters, most of whom had settled on the grant after the discovery of gold. Some Mexicans had difficulty establishing ownership despite the fact that they lived upon land where their fathers had lived before them. Involvement by the" Santa Fe Ring" intensified the entire situation with legal and political manipulation.

Ultimately engaged to defend the company, a young lawyer by the name of Frank Springer moved to Cimarron in time to, first, successfully defend McMains against charges of murder, then to become chief counsel for the Maxwell Land Grant Company in its fight against anti-granters.

On July 4, 1876, the country celebrated its first centennial birthday and Colorado was admitted to the Union. Slaves had been emancipated; the women's suffrage movement had begun; and thousands attending the Philadelphia Exposition heard the liberty bell toll. But no one in Philadelphia believed that Custer had been defeated at the Battle of Little Big Horn.

Within two years of Maxwell's death, the official Elkins-Marmon Survey, John Elkins being Steve Elkins' brother, measured over one million seven hundred thousand acres in the Beaubien and Miranda Grant, close to two thousand six hundred eighty square miles.

The United States Supreme Court ruled on the Sangre de Cristo Grant in the case of *John G.Tameling v. The United States Freehold and Emigration Company* that "Congress acted upon the claim as recommended by the Surveyor General. The Confirmation being absolute and unconditional without limitation as to quantity . . . , we must regard it as effectual, and operative for the entire tract."[58] Upon this case rested the later confirmation of the Maxwell Grant's boundaries.

On December 23, 1876, the Maxwell Land Grant and Railway Company was delinquent in payment of property tax. M.M. Mills paid almost sixteen thousand five hundred dollars at the tax sale for the conditional title of the Grant, and seven months later sold it to Thomas Catron for twenty thousand dollars. Foiling the efforts of Catron's Santa

Fe group, the company's Dutch bondholders managed to act before the legal period of redemption passed. Meeting the deadline that allowed debtors to buy back property sold for non-payment of taxes, the Maxwell Land Grant and Railway company paid Catron almost twenty-one thousand dollars to retain the title.[59]

Within three years after Maxwell's death, at least two dozen men died in Colfax County from other than natural causes, eight murdered and sixteen following brawls, in only one year's time.[60]

As war raged in Colfax County, another conflict developed farther south; the Lincoln County War lasted another three years. Violence and crime reigned. "Cattle rustling was so common as to be looked upon by many as no offense at all. Horse theft, although much more objectionable, was almost as routine."[61] Out of a conflict between men for money and power, a young outlaw named William Bonney rose to hero status as Billy the Kid; and President Hayes declared the area to be in a "state of insurrection."

After nearly twenty years of bargaining, all of the Utes in New Mexico were moved to one reservation in Colorado. The Moache Utes eventually settled on their own present lands in southwestern Colorado.[62] They share with the Capote Utes a reservation approximately fifteen miles wide by seventy-three miles long.[63]

Just short of four years after Maxwell's death, on May 19, 1879, Land Commissioner Williamson issued patents of ownership to the Maxwell Land Grant and Railway Company.

The Atchison, Topeka, and Santa Fe Railroad's tracks extended southward into New Mexico as far as Las Vegas; but it bypassed the little town of Cimarron where the Maxwell Land Grant and Railway Company, unable to make annual interest payments of three hundred fifty thousand dollars, was bankrupt and in foreclosure.

7

THE RIVER OF TIME
THE 1880S AND THEREAFTER

Five years after Lucien Maxwell's death, at nine in the morning on Monday, March 22, people gathered in front of Cimarron's City Hall to attend a sheriff's auction. For one million one hundred thousand dollars Frank Sherwin and Lucien Birdseye purchased first and second mortgage interests to become owners of the Maxwell Grant, incorporated the Maxwell Land Grant Company under laws of the United Netherlands, and issued bonds worth a million English pounds.

The Atchison, Topeka, and Santa Fe Railroad reached the Rio Grande and replaced forever the old Santa Fe Trail. Bypassing Santa Fe, it stopped at Lamy, seventeen miles away, from which tracks were built by the Denver and Rio Grande Company to connect the train to its named destination of Santa Fe.

Raton began as a town, established on the site along the Santa Fe Trail known as Willow Springs.

Six years after Lucien Maxwell died, on the night of July 14, Pat Garrett shot escaped murderer Bill Bonney at Pete Maxwell's home in Fort Sumner. Today, when admirers visit Billy the Kid's grave, they wonder who could be buried under the nearby six-foot-high tombstone.

The Mississippi River changed course, flooding Kaskaskia, Illinois, for the last time. The town disappeared into the river. Pierre Menard's home, high on the bluff, survived and ultimately became a state museum.

Nine years after Lucien Maxwell's death, the Fort Sumner land title was finally cleared. Cattlemen bought the ranch and Luz homesteaded on neighboring land to start "new" Fort Sumner.

Twelve years after Lucien Maxwell's death, the Supreme Court of the United States confirmed in Miranda and Beaubien and their grantees the patent previously issued by the government of the United States for the acreage originally claimed by Lucien.

Fourteen years after Lucien Maxwell's death, only five hundred fifty-one American buffalo remained of the over twenty million that had roamed the prairies in 1850.

Eighteen years after Lucien Maxwell's death, open range came to an end and "old" Fort Sumner was abandoned. By the turn of the century the buildings were gone, many having been dismantled for use in homes as far as fifty miles away.[1]

Nineteen years after Lucien Maxwell's death, the Supreme Court of New Mexico ended the lawsuit brought by Alfred Bent's widow and heirs, denying any claim of fraud or imposition by Lucien Maxwell in connection with title conveyed.

Twenty-three years after Lucien Maxwell's death, his son Pete died and was buried at Fort Sumner.

Twenty-five years after Lucien Maxwell's death, his widow, Luz, died. Her oldest grandson, twenty-six-year-old Lieutenant Maxwell Keyes, with an already distinguished military record, had been dead seven months, killed in the service of his country at Ildefonso, Luzon, in the Philippines.

Thirty years after Lucien Maxwell's death, the railroad finally reached the Pecos River and a third town of Fort Sumner came into existence seven miles to the south.

Thirty-seven years after Lucien Maxwell's death, New Mexico gained admittance as forty-seventh state of the Union.

Forty years after Lucien Maxwell's death, his oldest daughter, Virginia, died one week before her father's birthday.

Forty-seven years after Lucien Maxwell's death, the Cimarron house burned to the ground.

Forty-nine years after Lucien Maxwell's death, the United States of America recognized automatic citizenship of Indians.

Fifty-two years after Lucien Maxwell's death, Frank Springer died. He had been involved in management of the Maxwell Land Grant for fifty-four years.

Also, Deluvina Maxwell died, having lived after Luz's death

with the Abreú family. Even in her last days, the old Navajo woman liked to tell of "Tata Makey" taking out a chunk of gold from his desk drawer to buy her from the Apaches who had taken her captive after killing her father and mother.[2]

Fifty-four years after Lucien Maxwell's death, the mortgage on the Maxwell Land Grant Company was satisfied and the trustees discharged.

Sixty years after Lucien Maxwell's death , Odile, his last surviving child, died.

Sixty-three years after Lucien Maxwell's death, Waite Phillips, owner of land that had been part of the original Beaubien and Miranda Grant, donated significant acreage to the Boy Scouts of America to begin Philmont Scout Ranch.

Seventy-two years after Lucien Maxwell's death, a federal mandate assured the right to vote to all American Indians.

Seventy-three years after Lucien Maxwell's death, granddaughter Adelina Welborn related a story about her grandfather to writer Joel Heflin Smith. She told of her Aunt Virginia and Captain Keyes in Arizona with their baby who needed milk. Their offer to buy a cow was refused by a man who wanted to keep his animals in a time of scarcity. But, when the man found out that Keyes was Lucien Maxwell's son-in-law, he "told him to take the pick of the cows." The man remembered, according to Adelina's mother, Paulita, that, "years before, he was coming through Maxwell's country with his family. Their teams were poor and they had no food. They stopped at the Manor House and granddad gave them food and fattened their teams."[3]

Seventy-four years after Lucien Maxwell's death, a new monument at Fort Sumner's cemetery honored Lucien Maxwell.

Ninety-two years after Lucien Maxwell's death, Virginia Maxwell's youngest child died, seventy-eight-year-old Geoffrey Keyes, graduate of West Point, Commander of first the Seventh Army and later the Third Army in postwar Germany, described by General George Patton as "the only officer that I have ever rated 'Superior' in all categories." Thoughts about Geoffrey Keyes could have been expressed one hundred years earlier about his grandfather and twenty-five years before that about his great-great-grandfather Pierre Menard. The 1973 West Point Alumni Magazine reported:

He gained loyalty and respect on the basis of his own ability and integrity, never relying on rank. He used a keen sense of humor to make others feel comfortable or to relieve tension, never at the expense of others' feelings or dignity. He had the courage to show compassion, and over the years he earned the devoted friendship of many, in high stations and low, not because he courted them but because they were drawn to him.[4]

Exactly 121 years after Lucien's death, at three-thirty in the afternoon on Thursday, July 25, 1996, black clouds gathered and descended through Cimarron Canyon, wind and rain whirling into a deadly funnel cloud. The tornado left an angry path, demolishing the post office and lifting roofs; but not one of the town's eight hundred citizens died.

8

WHAT'S LEFT?

One hundred fifty years ago seems like a very long time, but footprints of the past linger. On a warm Sunday afternoon in October 1994 Lucien Maxwell's granddaughter sat across from me at her kitchen table in Albuquerque, New Mexico. Eighty-three years old, Stella talked of the old days in Fort Sumner, about her mother Odile, whose sixth birthday was shadowed by Lucien Maxwell's death. Stella's son, Manuel, showed me newspaper clippings about "The Duke of Cimarron."

The day before, on the eastern side of the Sangre de Cristos, I sat in the living room of another house, some fifty miles south of Cimarron. The next generation of Maxwell descendants, son and granddaughters of Stella's nephew, shared a chart of their family's history. Births, deaths, and marriages of Menards, Beaubiens, and Maxwells. I knew, sitting next to the handsome, dark-haired man, that my quest for Lucien Maxwell, though reaching into the past, would bring me to the present.

The Santa Fe Trail was ultimately replaced by railroad tracks and powerful steam-run engines, but deep wagon ruts, even today, mark its path. Treaty-making Americans uprooted Utes and Jicarilla Apaches, but sacred places remain, hidden among snow-covered mountains high above Cimarron. With each decade, displaced and replaced remnants of the past merge into a new shape that will be the future.

New Mexico's dinosaur tracks tell of prehistoric animals and drawings of concentric circles indicate a human presence many thousand years ago. The earth has changed as have its occupants, becoming at the end of their lives part of the planet that sustained them. Even stone monuments ultimately disappear, but each succeeding generation carries forward dreams of the past.

The carriers of the dreams are people like Luz and Lucien Maxwell, willing travelers to unruled, new frontiers, where new land nurtures new ideas, tested by reality as opposed to authority. Lucien Maxwell was a builder; he worked with and used the land. Married to a woman of mixed French-Canadian and Hispanic family roots, raised by a father and a grandfather who had lived and dealt and traded with Indians, schooled in strong Catholic traditions that allowed him to be a part of New Mexico's Catholic culture, Lucien Maxwell built a community that bridged boundaries.

One hundred fifty years have erased much of the physical evidence of his life. A flooding Pecos River washed away whatever markers were left at Fort Sumner's military cemetery where he and Luz were buried. The present-day monument was erected in 1949 by the Colorado State Historical Society. Legends have grown bigger than the men who are buried there, Lucien Maxwell bearing the brunt of what happened after his departure from Cimarron and William "Billy the Kid" Bonney receiving the glory of the west. Both took the law into their own hands, one to build and the other to kill. Frank Silva, living today in Fort Sumner, proudly carries the name and the stories of his grandfather who knew both men.

Of the three houses in New Mexico where Lucien Maxwell and his family lived, only the Rayado house remains, now part of Philmont Scout Ranch.

Atop the hill by the Cimarron River an iron fence surrounds two graves that thus far lie undisturbed on private property. Writing on stone markers records the dates of their lives, three-year-old Verenisa Maxwell and her grandmother, Pabla Beaubien. Across the road and past the meadow stands the three-story mill, its water-carrying flume long dry but its gears intact and grinding stones seemingly only at rest from the last flour-making day when Utes and Apaches gathered outside its walls.

Communities change; countries change; even mountains and skies change. The lands of the Beaubien-Miranda Grant have been sold and resold many times since Lucien Maxwell's transfer of title. Title is now secure, at least as far as the courts are concerned, though grant and anti-grant feelings are yet carried by descendants of those who were there one hundred twenty-five years ago. Residents of Beaubien's other grant, the Sangre de Cristo, at the time of this writing, are yet fighting for rights they claim were promised their ancestors by Don Carlos.

Lucien and Luz Beaubien Maxwell left their lands; but, because New Mexico is truly the Land of Enchantment, the Cimarron country still bears their imprint. Yes, newer buildings have been built and different people walk there; but towering mountains still stretch haughtily into clear blue skies. Precious water yet flows from their peaks, greening the western edge of the Great Plains. Today, Lucien Maxwell's mill still stands, tallest structure for miles around, reminding us of the dreams of a blue-eyed Illinois boy.

NOTES

CHAPTER 1: THE VECTORS CONVERGE

1. E.J. Montague, *Historical Sketches of Randolph County* (Alton, Ill: Courier Steam Book and Job Printing Press, 1859), 47-48.

2. Louis Houck, *History of Missouri*, 3 vols. (Chicago: R.R.Donnelly and Sons, 1908), 2:305, quoted in Lawrence Murphy, *Lucien Bonaparte Maxwell* (Norman: University of Oklahoma Press, 1983), 8.

3. State of Illinois Historic Site Audio/Visual Presentation, "Pierre Menard Home," (Fort Gage, Ill., 1991).

4. Josiah Gregg, *Commerce of the Prairies*, ed. Max Moorhead (1844; reprint, Norman: University of Oklahoma Press, 1991), 13-16.

5. Henry Inman, *The Old Santa Fe Trail* (1897; reprint, New York: The Macmillan Co., 1981), 266-67.

6. Montague, *Historical Sketches*, 38.

7. Jan Pettit, *Utes: The Mountain People*, rev. ed. (Boulder: Johnson Books, 1990), 99.

8. Richard N. Ellis, *New Mexico Past and Present A Historical Reader* (Albuquerque: University of New Mexico Press, 1971), 112.

9. Gregg, *Commerce of the Prairies*, 30.

10. Richard Oglesby, "Pierre Menard," in *The Mountain Men and Fur Trade of the Far West*, ed. Leroy R. Hafen (Glendale, Calif.: The Arthur H. Clarke Co., 1968), 6:316.

11. Ibid., 314-15.

12. Pierre Menard Home Historic Site.

13. Oglesby, "Pierre Menard," 314.

14. Montague, *Historical Sketches*, 39.

CHAPTER 2: ADOLESCENCE FOR LUCIEN AND FOR AMERICA

1. Paul Johnson, *The Birth of the Modern* (New York: Harper Collins Publishers, 1991), 873-75.

2. Lois Carrier, *Illinois: Crossroads of a Continent* (Urbana: University of Illinois Press, 1993), 52, 57.

3. Ibid., 76, 69-70.

4. J.F. Snyder, "The Old French Towns of Illinois in 1839," *Journal of Illinois State Historical Society* 36 (1943): 353-54.

5. Ibid., 356.

6. Ibid., 355, 357, 360-1.

7. Ibid., 357-62.

8. Ibid., 359-60.

9. Dumas Malone, ed., "Michel Branamour Menard," *Dictionary of American Biography* (New York: Scribner's, 1933), 6:528.

10. David Lavender, *Bent's Fort* (Lincoln: University of Nebraska Press, 1954), 150-53.

11. Murphy, *Lucien Bonaparte Maxwell*, 19.

12. John Rybolt, ed., *The American Vincentians* (Brooklyn: New City Press, 1988), 293.

13. William Clark Kennerly (1824-1912) quoted in Rybolt, *The American Vincentians*, 293.

14. John E. Sunder, *Bill Sublette Mountain Man* (Norman: University of Oklahoma Press, 1959), 175, 238.

15. Ray Allen Billington, *Westward Expansion*, 4th ed. (New York: Macmillan Publishing, 1974), 385.

16. Inman, *The Old Santa Fe Trail*, 268-69.

17. Stanley Vestal, *Joe Meek: Mountain Man* (1952, reprint, Lincoln: University of Nebraska Press, 1963), 15.

18. Carrier, *Illinois: Crossroads of a Continent*, 81.

19. Vestal, *Joe Meek*, 239.

20. W. Eugene Hollon, *The Southwest Old and New* (Lincoln: University of Nebraska Press, 1961), 271.

21. Saint Mary's of the Barrens, Perryville, Missouri, Accounts of Saint Mary's College, 1833-1837, File # A108.

CHAPTER 3: COMING OF AGE

1. Susan Magoffin, *Down the Santa Fe Trail and into Mexico: The Diary of Susan Shelby Magoffin*, 1846-1847, ed. Stella Drumm (1926, Reprint, New Haven: Yale University Press, 1962), 60.

2. Lavender, *Bent's Fort*, 145-48.

3. Bill Gilbert, *Westering Man: The Life Of Joseph Walker* (New York: Atheneum, 1983), 155.

4. John William Grassham, "Charles H. Beaubien, 1800-1864" (Master's Thesis, New Mexico State University, 1983), viii.

5. William Keleher, *The Maxwell Land Grant*, 2nd ed. Albuquerque: University of New Mexico Press, 1964), 26.

6. Murphy, *Lucien Bonaparte Maxwell*, 37.

7. Charles Preuss, *Exploring with Fremont: The Private Diaries of Charles Preuss . . .* , 6-7, referred to in Lawrence Murphy, *Lucien Bonaparte Maxwell*, 40.

8. John C. Fremont, *Report of the Exploring Expedition to the Rocky Mountains in the Year 1842* (Washington: Gales and Seaton, 1845), 27-30.

9. Gilbert, *Westering Man*, 185.

10. Gregg, *Commerce of the Prairies*, 68.

11. Ibid., 98-103.

12. Ibid., 107-110.

13. Ibid., 144-46.

14. Mamie Harris Engel, granddaughter of Pablo and Rebecca Abreú Beaubien, interview by John William Grassham, "Charles H. Beaubien," 11.

15. Ibid., viii.

16. Victor Westphall, *Mercedes Reales: Hispanic Land Grants of the Upper Rio Grande Region*, (Albuquerque: University of New Mexico Press, 1982), 3.

17. Ibid., 10.

18. Grassham, "Charles H. Beaubien," 52, and Lawrence R. Murphy, "The Beaubien and Miranda Land Grant, 1841-1846," *New Mexico Historical Review* (42: January, 1967), 31-2. Some authorities have questioned the possibility of all seven rock mounds having been erected in the time specified and where later indicated by Maxwell at the time of the survey.

19. Westphall, *Mercedes Reales*, 48.

20. Ibid., 36,44, 285-6.

21. Veronica E. Velarde Tiller, *The Jicarilla Apache Tribe* (Lincoln: University of Nebraska Press, 1983), 10.

22. John L. O'Sullivan, *United States Magazine and Democratic Review* (July-Aug, 1845) wrote of "our manifest destiny to overspread the continent allotted by Providence for the free development of our yearly multiplying millions."

23. Hubert Howe Bancroft, *History of Arizona and New Mexico* (1889; facsimile edition, Albuquerque: Horn and Wallace, 1962), 417.

24. Edwin L. Sabin, *Kit Carson Days* (rev. edition, Lincoln: University of Nebraska Press, 1995), 2:512-15.

25. Janet Lecompte, *Pueblo, Hardscrabble, Greenhorn* (Norman: University of Oklahoma Press, 1978), 194.

26. Lewis H. Garrard, *Wah-to-yah* (1850; reprint, Norman: University of Oklahoma Press, 1955), 119.

27. Ibid., 132.

28. Ibid., 143, 177, 176.

29. Lavender, 316.

30. Lawrence Murphy, "Rayado," *New Mexico Historical Review* 46 no.1 (1971), 38.

31. Grassham, "Charles H. Beaubien," 41.

32. Lecompte, *Pueblo, Hardscrabble, Greenhorn*, 238.

33. Janet Lecompte, "The Manco Burro Pass Massacre," *New Mexico Historical Review* 41 no.4 (1966), 313-14.

34. Ibid., 313-14. The two children were kidnapped by the Indians and within a few months ransomed and returned.

35. Thelma S. Guild and Harvey L. Carter, *Kit Carson* (Lincoln: University of Nebraska Press, 1984), 182-3.

36. Harvey L. Carter, *'Dear Old Kit'* (Norman: University of Oklahoma Press, 1968), 123.

37. Leonard Pitt, *The Decline of the Californios* (Berkeley: University of California Press, 1966), 40, 52.

38. David Reynolds, *Walt Whitman's America* (New York: Alfred Knopf, 1995), 221.

39. Ibid., 108-9.

40. William Walker, *Transcript of Record of Charles Bent et als. v. Guadalupe Miranda et als.*, 255. Hereinafter cited as *Bent v. Miranda*.

41. Louisa Ward Arps, "From Trading Post to Melted Adobe, 1849-1920," *The Colorado Magazine*, 54 no.4, (1977), reprint by the University Press of Colorado, (1992), 31 nn.1-6. Debate continues as to whether Bent blew up the fort and burned it. See James H. Baker and Leroy Hafen, eds., *History of Colorado*, 5 vols. (Denver: Linderman, Co., 1927), 1:318 n.83; David Lavender, *Bent's Fort* (Garden City, N.Y.: Doubleday and Co., 1954), 313-16.

CHAPTER 4: RAYADO

1. "The Rayado Ranch of Colfax County, New Mexico," *National Register of Historic Places*, Section E, 9, Section 7, 3-4.

2. Sabin, *Kit Carson Days*, 626-27.

3. Anna P. Hannum, ed., *A Quaker Forty-Niner: The Adventures of Charles Edward Pancoast on the American Frontier* (Philadelphia: University of Pennsylvania Press, 1930), 208-9, quoted in Murphy, *Lucien Bonaparte Maxwell*, 87.

4. William Walker, Testimony Maxwell Case *Transcript*, 59, 62, 72, quoted in Lawrence Murphy, "Rayado," 40; *Bent v. Miranda*, 225.

5. George A. McCall, *New Mexico in 1850: A Military View*, ed. Robert W. Frazer (Norman: University of Oklahoma Press, 1968), 145-50.

6. Carter, *Dear Old Kit*, 124.

7. Gregg, *Commerce of the Prairies*, 114.

8. Sabin, *Kit Carson Days*, 631.

9. Ibid.

10. Herbert Pickens Gambrell, "Michel Branamour Menard," Menard Collection, Rosenberg Library of Galveston, Texas.

11. Edward S. Ellis, *The Life of Kit Carson* (New York: Mershon Co., 1889), 221.

12. Lecompte, *Pueblo, Hardscrabble, Greenhorn*, 229.

13. Howard Lewis Conard, *Uncle Dick Wootton* (Chicago: The Lakeside Press, 1957), 264; Thelma S. Guild and Carter, *Kit Carson*, 194, says $5.50; Sabin, *Kit Carson Days*, 634, says "no more than $2.50 a head."

14. Irving Stone, *Men to Match My Mountains* (Garden City, N.Y.: Doubleday and Co., Inc., 1956), 163-66.

15. Pitt, *The Decline of the Californios*, 121, 123-24.

16. Guild and Carter, *Kit Carson*, 197.

17. *Act to Regulate Trade and Intercourse with the Indian Tribes and to Preserve the Peace on the Frontiers*, June 30, 1934, quoted in Dee Brown, *Bury My Heart at Wounded Knee* (New York: Holt, Rinehart and Winston, 1970), 6.

18. Donald C. Cutter, "An Inquiry into Indian Land Rights . . . with Particular Reference to the Jicarilla Apache Area of Northeastern New Mexico," in *Apache Indians* vol. 6, American Indian Ethnohistory Series (New York: Garland Publishing Co., 1974), 245-80, quoted in Tiller, *The Jicarilla Apache Tribe*, 10.

19. Lecompte, *Pueblo, Hardscrabble, Greenhorn*, 238-39.

20. Tiller, *The Jicarilla Apache Tribe*, 37.

21. Ibid., 47, 56.

22. *Santa Fe Weekly Gazette* April 8, 1854, quoted in Murphy, "Rayado," 51.

23. Dr. Dewitt Peters, *Kit Carson's Life and Adventures* (Hartford: Dustin, Gilman and Co., 1874), 334-35.

24. Lawrence Murphy, *Philmont* (Albuquerque: University of New Mexico Press, 1972), 69.

25. *Transcript of Title*, 31, 35, 36, quoted in Murphy, *Lucien Bonaparte Maxwell*, 103.

26. Hollon, *The Southwest Old and New*, 209-10; Wells Fargo Museum, Los Angeles, California.

27. Stone, *Men to Match My Mountains*, 192.

28. *Denver Rocky Mountain News Daily*, January 1, 1873, 4, quoted in Lecompte, *Pueblo, Hardscrabble, Greenhorn*, 256.

29. Stone, *Men to Match My Mountains*, 208.

30. Tiller, *Jicarilla Apache Tribe*, 14.

CHAPTER 5: CIMARRON

1. *Annual Reports of the Commissioner of the General Land Office of the United States* October 22, 1985, 49 Cong., 1 Sess. House of Executive Document no. 1, 277-78(2378), quoted in Victor Westphall, *Mercedes Reales*, 49.

2. William A. Bell, *New Tracks in North America* (1870; reprint, Albuquerque: Calvin Horn, 1965), 108.

3. Inman, *Old Santa Fe Trail*, 374.

4. Ibid., 147.

5. Ibid., 155.

6. Ibid., 376.

7. Calvin Jones, *Bent v. Miranda*, 155.

8. Inman, *Old Santa Fe Trail*, 377.

9. Brown, *Bury My Heart at Wounded Knee*, 199.

10. Maxwell to Edmond Menard, November 11, 1912, Pierre Menard Collection, Illinois State Historical Library, Roll 9, Frame 35.

11. Senate, "Sand Creek Massacre," *Report of the Secretary of War*, Sen. Exec. Doc.26, 39 Cong., 2 sess. Washington, G.P.O., 1867., v, quoted in Stan Hoig, *The Sand Creek Massacre* (Norman: University of Oklahoma, 1963), 168.

12. Herbert O. Brayer, *William Blackmore: The Spanish-Mexican Land Grants of New Mexico and Colorado, 1863-1878*, 1949; reprint, Carlos E. Cortes ed., *The Mexican American* (New York: Arno Press, 1974), 65-67.

13. Jesus Abreú, *Bent v. Miranda*, 279.

14. Beaubien and Miranda to Bent, March 2, 1843, Day Book A, Register of Land Claims Under the Kearny Code, 1847, U.S. Bureau of Land Management Archives, Santa Fe, cited in Murphy, *Lucien Bonaparte Maxwell*, 106. At the same time, Beaubien and Miranda deeded New Mexico Governor Armijo a similar one-fourth interest. Nothing resulted from any claims made by him or his heirs. See Murphy, "The Beaubien and Miranda Land Grant 1841-1846," *New Mexico Historical Review* 42 (January, 1967), 32.

15. Calvin Jones, *Bent v. Miranda*, 164.

16. *The Santa Fe New Mexican* (August 12, 1864), quoted in Lawrence Murphy, "Master of the Cimarron," *New Mexico Historical Review* 55:1 (1980), 7.

17. William Hoehne, Arthur Morrison, *Bent v. Miranda*, 364, 379-80.

18. *Denver Daily Rocky Mountain News*, February 14, 1866, quoted in Murphy, *Lucien Bonaparte Maxwell*, 113.

19. A.B. Norton to D.N. Cooley, September 28, 1866, in *Annual Report of the Commissioner of Indian Affairs, 1866*, Senate Executive Document No. 1, 144-5, quoted in Murphy, *Lucien Bonaparte Maxwell*, 136. William Keleher, *Maxwell Land Grant*, cites additional correspondence of August 27, 1867, from Norton to N.G. Taylor, Commissioner of Indian Affairs, Washington City, D.C., in the 1967 "Report of the Acting Commissioner of Indian Affairs."

20. Marcus Brunswick, *Bent v. Miranda*, 320.

21. William Keleher, *Turmoil in New Mexico:1846 -1868* (Santa Fe: Rydal Press, 1952), 383.

22. James Jefferson, Robert Delaney, and Gregory C. Thompson, *The Southern Utes A Tribal History*, 2nd ed. (Ignacio, Colo.: Southern Ute Tribe, 1972), 22.

23. Guild and Carter, *Kit Carson*, 267.

24. Paul Horgon, *Lamy of Santa Fe* (New York: Farrar, Straus and Giroux, 1975), 345-48.

25. Keleher, *Turmoil*, 409-20.

26. A.B. Norton, in *New Mexico Indian Letters*, Microcopy #234, Roll

553 N.A. Copy in the Old Mill Museum, Cimarron, New Mexico.

27. William Keleher, *The Fabulous Frontier* (1945, revised, Albuquerque: University of New Mexico Press, 1962), 74.

28. Calvin Jones, *Bent v. Miranda*, 157.

29. Bell, *New Tracks*, 109.

30. Inman, *Old Santa Fe Trail*, 374.

31. Ibid., 376.

32. Irving Howbert, *Memories of a Lifetime in the Pike's Peak Region* (1925; reprint, Glorietta, New Mexico: Rio Grande Press, 1970), 169, quoted in Murphy, "Master of the Cimarron," 13.

33. Inman, *Old Santa Fe Trail*, 378-79.

34. Ibid., 379-80.

35. Jim Berry Pearson, *The Maxwell Land Grant* (Norman: University of Oklahoma Press, 1961), 21-22.

36. Ibid., 24-26.

37. Inman, *Old Santa Fe Trail*, 378.

38. Chuck Hornung, *Raton (New Mexico) Range*, September 12, 1971, recounting from *The Santa Fe New Mexican*, April 23, 1864.

39. Andrew Calhoun, *Bent v. Miranda*, 106.

40. Thomas Hart, Daniel Taylor, Calvin Jones, *Bent v. Miranda*. 116-17, 133, 159.

41. *Bent v. Miranda*, 117.

42. Ibid., 133.

43. Ibid., 159, 162.

44. Adelina Welborn quoted in Joe Heflin Smith, "The Unmarked Grave," *The Cattleman* (May, 1949), 20.

45. *Bent v. Miranda*, 248-49.

46. Ibid., 254-56.

47. Keleher, *Maxwell Land Grant*, 31.

48. William Walker, *Bent v. Miranda*, 254-55.

49. Sytha Motto, *Old Houses of New Mexico and the People who Built Them* (Albuquerque: Calvin Horn Publishers, Inc., 1972), 52-54.

50. Ibid., 56-57.

51. Ibid., 60-61.

52. *Santa Fe New Mexican* (April 23, 1864), quoted in Murphy, "Master of the Cimarron," 13.

53. Agnes Morley Cleaveland, *Satan's Paradise* (Boston: Houghton Mifflin Company, 1952), 7-8.

54. Pearson, *Maxwell Land Grant*, 47-48.

55. Sabin, *Kit Carson Days*, 808-809.

56. George Bird Grinnell, *The Fighting Cheyennes* (1915; reprint, Williamstown, Mass.: Corner House Publishers, 1976), 298.

57. Howard Roberts Lamar, *The Far Southwest 1846-1912* (New Haven: Yale University Press, 1966), 142.

58. *Santa Fe Gazette* (March 13, 1869), quoted in Murphy, *Lucien Bonaparte Maxwell*, 164.

59. Marc Simmons, *New Mexico: A Bicentennial History* (New York: W.W. Norton and Co., Inc., 1977), 156.

60. J. Evetts Haley, *Charles Goodnight: Cowman and Plainsman* (Norman: University of Oklahoma Press, 1936), 212-13.

61. John Collinson and William Bell, *The Maxwell Land Grant* (London: Taylor and Cox, 1870), 27-28, quoted in Murphy, *Lucien Bonaparte Maxwell*, 161.

62. J.C. Furnas, *The Americans* (New York: G.P. Putnam's Sons, 1969), 668.

63. Lamar, *The Far Southwest*, 139.

64. Thomas Harwood, *History of New Mexico Spanish and English Missions* (Albuquerque: El Abogado Press, 1908), 67.

CHAPTER 6: FORT SUMNER ON THE PECOS

1. Pearson, *Maxwell Land Grant*, 48-49.

2. Murphy, *Lucien Bonaparte Maxwell*, 144.

3. Harwood, *History of New Mexico*, 85-86.

4. Geoffrey B. Keyes, telephone conversation with author, April 1996.

5. Pearson, *Maxwell Land Grant*, 50.

6. Marcus Brunswick, *Bent v. Miranda*, 321; Jack D. Rittenhouse, *The Man Who Owned Too Much* (Houston: Stagecoach Press, 1958), 49.

7. Adelina Welborn, quoted in Smith, "Unmarked Grave," 68.

8. Marcus Brunswick in *Bent v. Miranda*, 322, says one hundred fifty thousand, but Murphy in *Lucien Bonaparte Maxwell*, 189, says one hundred twenty-five thousand. Both say only fifty thousand in cash.

9. Some sources say they left the following spring; but if Virginia's first child was born at Fort Sumner as Murphy, in his extremely reliable *Lucien Bonaparte Maxwell*, 148, indicates, then they left in the autumn of 1871.

10. Victor Westphall, *The Public Domain in New Mexico, 1854-1891*, (Albuquerque: University of New Mexico Press, 1865), 68.

11. Stone, *Men to Match My Mountains*, 360.

12. Chuck Hornung, *Raton (New Mexico) Range*, September 5, 1971.

13. Hoehne, *Bent v. Miranda*, 368-73.

14. Lecompte, *Pueblo, Hardscrabble, Greenhorn*, 258-60.

15. William F. Shamleffer, "Merchandising Sixty Years Ago," *Kansas State Historical Society Collections* (Topeka: Kansas State Printing Plant, 1925), 16: 567-59, quoted in David Dary, *Entrepreneurs of the Old West* (New York: Alfred Knopf, 1986), 181.

16. Paul A.F. Walter, "New Mexico's Pioneer Bank and Bankers," *New Mexico Historical Review* 21 (1946), 216.

17. *Las Vegas Gazette*, November 25, 1875, quoted in Keleher, *Fabulous Frontier*, 35, 61.

18. Mrs. Michel Nalda, quoted in James D. Shinkle, *Fort Sumner and the Bosque Redondo* (Roswell, N. Mex.: Hall-Poorbaugh Press, 1965), 80-81; Keleher, *Maxwell Land Grant*, 36.

19. According to Victor Westphall, *Public Domain in New Mexico*, 86-87: "Lucien purchased buildings and improvements on the abandoned military reservation and, together with some forty families, moved there to live. In 1872 Maxwell, through his attorney, J. Houghton of Santa Fe, requested permission to purchase the land within the limits of the reserve at private sale. He was informed that . . . he had no right to the land . . . [which] could be disposed of only in accordance with the provisions of the Act of February 24, 1871, which called for appraisal of the land and sale at public auction. . . . Most of the land in the Fort Sumner Military Reservation was eventually sold at public sale on January 15, 1884. . . . Fort Sumner was the only reservation reverting to the public domain by a Special Act of Congress."

20. The Reverend Thomas Harwood's *History of New Mexico*, 110-18, included "The Maxwell Romance," supposedly a reproduction of an article (no date mentioned) which had appeared in the *Denver Republican*, and his repudiation of some of the story told therein. He did not comment upon the statement that Maxwell met his newly married daughter in New York City, placed ten thousand dollars to her credit and separated from Virginia forever. The facts of Virginia's children's births and early years at Fort Sumner do prove otherwise.

21. Obituary of Maxwell Keyes, *Albuquerque Weekly News* (Albuquerque, New Mexico), December 9, 1899, vol 3, 4g.

22. Harwood, *History of New Mexico*, 88.

23. Keleher, *Fabulous Frontier*, xii.

24. Dary, *Entrepreneurs*, 303.

25. Howard Bryan, *Wildest of the West* (Santa Fe: Clear Light Publishers, 1988), 84.

26. Miguel Antonio Otero, *The Mexican American: An Autobiographical Trilogy* (1935; reprint New York: Arno Press, 1974), 1:157.

27. *Santa Fe Post*, April 25, 1871.

28. *Santa Fe Daily New Mexican*, January 12, 1872, quoted in Murphy, *Lucien Bonaparte Maxwell*, 200.

29. Dary, *Entrepreneurs*, 211.

30. Joel Jacobsen, *Such Men as Billy the Kid* (Lincoln: University of Nebraska Press, 1994), 27; Keleher, *Fabulous Frontier*, 58-59.

31. Dary, *Entrepreneurs*, 219.

32. James Marshall, *Santa Fe: the Railroad that Built an Empire* (New York: Random House, 1945), 69.

33. Dary, *Entrepreneurs*, 229, 231-32.

34. *Santa Fe Daily New Mexican*, February 18, 1872, quoted in Murphy, *Lucien Bonaparte Maxwell*, 199, 248. Although some sources maintain he in-

vested two hundred fifty thousand dollars in railroad bonds and lost it all when the company went bankrupt, this, according to Murphy, is a more likely scenario.

35. Marshall, *Santa Fe: the Railroad* (New York: Random House, 1945), 212.

36. Allan Nevins, *Fremont: Pathmarker of the West* (1939; reprint, New York: Longmans, Green and Co., 1955), 589-90, 591.

37. William Oliver, *Eight Months in Illinois* (Newcastle Upon Tyne: E. and T. Bruce, 1843), 19-21, quoted in M.H. Dunlop, *Sixty Miles From Contentment* (New York: Basic Books, 1995), 176.

38. Pearson, *Maxwell Land Grant*, 61.

39. Ibid., 63.

40. Ibid., 52, 59.

41. John Collinson and William Bell, *The Maxwell Land Grant, Situated in Colorado and New Mexico, United States of America* (London: Taylor and Co., 1870), 16-24, and *Santa Fe Daily New Mexican*, August 4, 1870, quoted in Murphy, *Lucien Bonaparte Maxwell*, 182.

42. Westphall, *Mercedes Reales*, 58-59.

43. Ibid., 49.

44. Brayer, *William Blackmore*, 19.

45. Westphall, *Mercedes Reales*, 94.

46. Lamar, *Far Southwest*, 138.

47. Brayer, *William Blackmore*, 18.

48. Victor Westphall, *Thomas Benton Catron* (Tucson: University of Arizona Press, 1973), 72.

49. Lamar, *Far Southwest*, 148.

50. Murphy, *Lucien Bonaparte Maxwell*, 169.

51. Ibid.

52. Lamar, *Far Southwest*, 144.

53. Donald Worcester, *The Apaches: Eagles of the Southwest* (Norman: University of Oklahoma Press, 1979), 141.

54. Presumably the writing of Louisa Beaubien Barrett, from notebook found in 1960 by later owners of the property where she once lived. From the private collection of H.R. Parsons, Fort Sumner, New Mexico.

55. Tiller, *Jicarilla Apache Tribe*, 77; Jefferson, *Southern Utes*, 32-33, 42; Keleher, *Maxwell Land Grant*, 61.

56. Keleher, *Maxwell Land Grant*, 76.

57. Ibid., 76.

58. Pearson, *Maxwell Land Grant*, 75-76.

59. Ibid., 74.

60. Ibid., 88.

61. Robert Utley, *High Noon in Lincoln: Violence on the Western Frontier* (Albuquerque: University of New Mexico Press, 1987), 173.

62. Jefferson, *Southern Utes*, 32-33, 41-42.

63. Charles S. Marsh, *People of the Shining Mountains* (Boulder, Colo.: Pruett Publishing, 1982), 123.

CHAPTER 7: THE RIVER OF TIME

1. Mrs. Michel Nalda, youngest daughter of Manuel and Odile Maxwell Abreú, and granddaughter of Luz and Lucien Maxwell, quoted in Shinkle, *Fort Sumner and the Bosque Redondo*, 82-85.

2. Louisa Beaubien Barrett.

3. Smith, "Unmarked Grave," 21.

4. *Assembly*, West Point Alumni Magazine, September 1973, 133.

BIBLIOGRAPHY

Albuquerque Weekly News. Albuquerque, New Mexico. December 9, 1899: 4:3g.

Arps, Louisa Ward. "From Trading Post to Melted Adobe, 1849-1920." *The Colorado Magazine* 54, no.4 (1977): 29-55. Reprint by the University of Colorado Press, 1994.

Assembly. West Point Alumni Magazine (September 1973), 133.

Bancroft, Hubert Howe. *History of Arizona and New Mexico.* 1889, facsimile ed., Albuquerque: Horn and Wallace, 1962.

Barrett, Louisa Beaubien. Notebook in private Collection. H.R. Parsons. Fort Sumner, New Mexico.

Basler, Lucille. *District of Ste Genevieve.* 2nd ed. Sainte Genevieve, Missouri, 1980.

Bell, William A. *New Tracks in North America.* 1870. Reprint, Albuquerque: Calvin Horn, 1965.

Billington, Ray Allen. *Westward Expansion.* 4th Edition. New York: Macmillan Publishing, 1974.

Brayer, Herbert O. *William Blackmore: The Spanish-Mexican Land Grants of New Mexico and Colorado, 1863-1878.* 1949. Reprint in *The Mexican American,* advisory ed. Carlos E. Cortes. New York: Arno Press, 1974.

Brown, Dee. *Bury My Heart at Wounded Knee.* New York: Holt, Rinehart and Winston, 1970.

Bryan, Howard. *Wildest of the Wild West.* Santa Fe: Clear Light Publishers, 1988.

Carman, Harry J. and Harold C. Syrett. *A History of the American People.* 2 vols. New York: Alfred A. Knopf, 1956.

Carrier, Lois. *Illinois: Crossroads of a Continent.* Urbana: University of Illinois Press, 1993.

Carter, Harvey Lewis. *Dear Old Kit.* Norman: University of Oklahoma Press, 1968.

_____ . "Lucien Maxwell." *Mountain Men and the Fur Trade of the Far West.* Vol. 6. Hafen, Leroy, ed. Glendale, Calif.: The Arthur H. Clark Co., 1968.

Cleaveland, Agnes Morley. *Satan's Paradise*. 1941. Reprint, Boston: Houghton Mifflin Co., 1952.

Conard, Howard Louis. *Uncle Dick Wootton*. Edited by Milo Milton Quaife. Chicago: Lakeside Press, R.R.Donnelly and Sons Co., 1957.

Dary, David. *Entrepreneurs of the Old West*. New York: Alfred Knopf, 1986.

Dunlop, M.H. *Sixty Miles From Contentment*. New York: Basic Books, 1995.

Ellis, Edward S. *The Life of Kit Carson*. New York: Mershon Co., 1889.

Ellis, Richard N., ed. *New Mexico Past and Present: A Historical Reader*. Albuquerque: University of New Mexico Press, 1971.

First National Bank of Santa Fe. Archives and Records.

Frémont, John Charles. *Narratives of Exploration and Adventure*. Edited by Allan Nevins. New York: Longmans, Green, and Co., 1956.

Furnas, J.C. *The Americans: A Social History of the United States, 1587-1914*. New York: G.P. Putnam's Sons, 1969.

Gambrell, Herbert Pickins. "Michel Branamour Menard." Menard Collection, Rosenberg Library, Galveston,Texas.

Garrard, Lewis H. *Wah-to-yah*. 1850. Reprinted from original, Norman: University of Oklahoma Press, 1955.

Gilbert, Bill. *Westering Man: The Life of Joseph Walker*. New York: Atheneum, 1983.

Grassham, John William. "Charles H. Beaubien, 1800-1864." Master's thesis, New Mexico State University, 1983.

Gregg, Josiah. *Commerce of the Prairies*. Edited by Max Moorhead. 1845. Norman: University of Oklahoma Press, 1954.

Grinnell, George Bird. *The Fighting Cheyennes*. 1915. Williamstown, Mass.: Corner House Publishers, 1976.

Guild, Thelma S. and Harvey Carter. *Kit Carson*. Lincoln: University of Nebraska, 1984.

Haley, J. Evetts. *Charles Goodnight*. 1936. Reprint, Norman: University of Oklahoma Press, 1949.

Harwood, Thomas. *History of New Mexico Spanish and English Missions of the Methodist Episcopal Church from 1850 to 1910*. Albuquerque: El Abogado Press, 1908.

Hoig, Stan. *The Sand Creek Massacre*. Norman: University of Oklahoma Press, 1963.

Hollon, W. Eugene. *The Southwest Old and New*. Lincoln: University of Nebraska Press, 1961.

Horgan, Paul. *Lamy of Santa Fe*. New York: Farrar, Straus and Giroux, 1975.

Hornung, Chuck. *Raton (New Mexico) Range*. September 12, 1971.

Inman, Henry. *The Old Santa Fe Trail*. 1897. Reprint, Norwood Press: Norwood, Massachusetts, 1981.

Jacobsen, Joel. *Such Men as Billy the Kid: The Lincoln County War Reconsidered*. Lincoln: University of Nebraska Press, 1994.

Jefferson, James; Robert Delaney; and Gregory C. Thompson. *The Southern Utes: A Tribal History*. 2nd ed. Ignacio, Colo.: Southern Ute Tribe, 1973.

Johnson, Paul. *The Birth of the Modern*. New York: Harper Collins Publishers, 1991.

Keleher, William A. *The Fabulous Frontier*. 1945. Revised ed., Albuquerque: University of New Mexico Press, 1962.

_____ . *Turmoil in New Mexico, 1846-1868*. Santa Fe: Rydal Press, 1952.

_____ . *The Maxwell Land Grant*. 1942. 2nd ed. New York: Argosy, 1964.

Lamar, Howard Roberts. *The Far Southwest, 1846-1912*. New Haven: Yale University Press, 1966.

Lavender, David. *Bent's Fort*. Lincoln: University of Nebraska Press, 1954.

Lecompte, Janet. *Pueblo, Hardscrabble, Greenhorn*. Norman: University of Oklahoma Press, 1978.

_____ . "The Manco Burro Pass Massacre." *New Mexico Historical Review* 41, no 4 (1966): 305-17.

Lyma, June and Norma Denier. *Ute People: An Historical Study*. Salt Lake City: University of Utah Press, 1970.

Magoffin, Susan. *Down the Santa Fe Trail and into Mexico: The Diary of Susan Shelby Magoffin, 1846-1847*. Stella M. Drumm, ed. 1926. Reprint, New Haven: Yale University Press, 1962.

Malone, Dumas, ed. "Michel Branamour Menard." *Dictionary of American Biography*. Vol. 6. New York: Scribner's, 1933.

Marsh, Charles S. *People of the Shining Mountains*. Boulder, Colo.: Pruett Publishing Co., 1982.

Marshall, James. *Santa Fe: The Railroad that Built an Empire*. New York: Random House, 1945.

McCall, Colonel George A. *New Mexico in 1850: A Military View*. Edited by Robert W. Frazer. Norman: University of Oklahoma Press, 1968.

Menard (Pierre) Collection, Illinois State Historical Library, Springfield.

Montague, E.J. *Historical Sketches of Randolph County*. Alton, Ill.: Courier Steam Book and Job Printing House, 1859.

Morris, Richard B. *Encyclopedia of American History*. 2 vols. New York: Harper and Brothers Publishers, 1953.

Morrison Papers. "Lucien Bonaparte Maxwell." Illinois State Historical Library, Springfield.

Motto, Sytha. *Old Houses of New Mexico and the People Who Built Them*. Albuquerque: Calvin Horn Publishers, Inc., 1972.

Murphy, Lawrence. *Lucien Bonaparte Maxwell*. Norman: University of Oklahoma Press, 1983.

_____ . "Beaubien and Miranda Land Grant 1841-1846." *New Mexico Historical Review* vol 42:2 (January, 1967), 27-47.

_____ . "Master of the Cimarron," *New Mexico Historical Review*. 55:1 (1980), 1-24.

_____ . "Rayado." *New Mexico Historical Review.* 46 (1971): 37-56.

_____ . *Philmont.* Albuquerque: University of New Mexico Press, 1972.

National Register of Historic Places. "The Rayado Ranch of Colfax County, New Mexico."

Nevins, Allan. *Frémont; Pathmarker of the West.* 1939. Reprint, New York: Longmans, Green and Co., 1955.

Norton, A.B. *New Mexico Indian Letters.* Microcopy #234, Row 553 N.A. Copy of letter re: purchase of land for reservation, October 10, 1866, in The Old Mill Museum, Cimarron, New Mexico.

Oglesby, Richard. "Pierre Menard." In *Mountain Men and the Fur Trade of the Far West.* Vol 6. Leroy Hafen, ed. Glendale, Calif.: The Arthur H. Clark Co., 1968.

Otero, Miguel Antonio. *The Mexican American.* 3 vols. 1935. Reprint of *My Life on the Frontier.* New York: Arno Press, 1974.

Pearson, Jim Berry. *The Maxwell Land Grant.* Norman: University of Oklahoma Press, 1961.

Peters, Dr. Dewitt. *The Life and Adventures of Kit Carson.* Hartford: Dustin, Gilman and Co., 1874.

Pettit, Jan. *Utes: The Mountain People.* Revised, Boulder: Johnson Books, 1990.

Pitt, Leonard. *The Decline of the Californios.* Berkeley: University of California Press, 1966.

Reeve, Agnesa Lufkin. *From Hacienda to Bungalow.* Albuquerque: University of New Mexico Press, 1988.

Reyling, August. *Historical Kaskaskia.* Saint Louis: 1963.

Reynolds, David S. *Walt Whitman's America.* New York: Alfred Knopf, 1995.

Rittenhouse, Jack D. *The Man Who Owned Too Much.* Reprint of "The Duke of Cimarron" from the *Saint Louis Globe Democrat,* July 21, 1895. Houston: Stagecoach Press, 1958.

Rybolt, John, ed. *The American Vincentians.* Brooklyn: New City Press, 1988.

Sabin, Edwin L. *Kit Carson Days.* 2 vols. 1935. Revised, Lincoln: University of Nebraska Press, 1995.

Saint Mary's of the Barrens, Perryville, Missouri. Accounts of Saint Mary's College, 1833-1837. File # A108.

Santa Fe Gazette. 6:9, August 13, 1861.

Santa Fe Post, April 25, 1871.

Shinkle, James D. *Fort Sumner and the Bosque Redondo.* Roswell, N. Mex.: Hall-Poorbaugh Press, 1965.

Simmons, Marc. *New Mexico: A Bicentennial History.* New York: W.W. Norton and Co., Inc., 1977.

Smith, Joe Heflin. "The Unmarked Grave." *The Cattleman* (May 1949), 19-20, 66-69.

Snyder, J.F. "The Old French Towns of Illinois in 1839." *Journal of Illinois State Historical Society.* 36 (1943): 345-367.

Stone, Irving. *Men to Match My Mountains*. Mainstream of America Series. Edited by Lewis Gannett. Garden City, N.Y.: Doubleday and Co., Inc., 1956.

Sunder, John E. *Bill Sublette: Mountain Man*. Norman: University of Oklahoma Press, 1959.

Tiller, Veronica E. Velarde. *The Jicarilla Apache Tribe*. Lincoln: University of Nebraska Press, 1983.

Transcript of Charles Bent et als. v. Guadalupe Miranda, et als. Supreme Court of the Territory of New Mexico, July Term, 1894.

Utley, Robert. *High Noon in Lincoln: Violence on the Western Frontier*. Albuquerque: University of New Mexico Press, 1987.

Vestal, Stanley. *Joe Meek: Mountain Man*. 1952. Reprint, Lincoln: University of Nebraska Press, 1963.

Walter, Paul A.F. "New Mexico's Pioneer Bank and Bankers." *New Mexico Historical Review* 21 (1946): 216.

Westphall, Victor. *Mercedes Reales: Hispanic Land Grants of the Upper Rio Grande Region*. Albuquerque: University of New Mexico Press, 1983.

_____ . *The Public Domain in New Mexico, 1854-1891*. Albuquerque: University of New Mexico Press, 1965.

_____ . *Thomas Benton Catron*. Tucson: University of Arizona Press, 1973.

Worcester, Donald E. *Eagles of the Southwest*. Norman: University of Oklahoma Press, 1979.

Zimmer, Stephen. Editor and compiler. *For Good Or Bad: People of the Cimarron Country*. Santa Fe: Sunstone Press, 1999.

AN APPRECIATION:

With special appreciation to the staff of both Philmont Museum, Cimarron, New Mexico, and Bud Werner Memorial Library, Steamboat Springs, Colorado.

HISTORICAL SITES VISITED:

Bent's Old Fort National Historic Site, Colorado
Chicago Historical Society
Cimarron Aztec Mill Museum
El Pueblo de Los Angeles Historic Monument
Kit Carson Home and Museum, Taos, New Mexico
Palace of the Governors, Santa Fe, New Mexico
Rayado Kit Carson Museum
Wells Fargo Museum, 333 South Grand Avenue, Los Angeles, California
Pierre Menard Home, Fort Gage, Illinois

INTERVIEWS WITH DESCENDANTS:

Les Davis, Cimarron, New Mexico, grandson of Frank Springer
Clarence Dennis ("Skip") Finley, Mora, New Mexico, great-grandson of Luz and Lucien's youngest daughter, Odile
Joe Finley, Albuquerque, New Mexico, grandson of Luz and Lucien's youngest daughter, Odile
Geoffrey Keyes, Pittsburgh, Pennsylvania, grandson of Luz and Lucien's oldest daughter, Virginia
Manuel Miller, Albuquerque, New Mexico, grandson of Luz and Lucien's youngest daughter, Odile
Stella Miller, Albuquerque, New Mexico, daughter of Luz and Lucien's youngest daughter, Odile
Frank Silva, Fort Sumner, New Mexico, grandson of Lucien Maxwell's *caporal*, Jesús Silva

INDEX

Keyes, Maxwell (grandson of LM), 115, 132
Keyes, Virginia. *See* Virginia Maxwell

Las Vegas, N.Mex., 37, 81, 115, 130
Lee, Robert E., 86, 110
Lee, Stephen Louis, 47
Lincoln, Abraham, 69, 70, 80, 81, 86, 101
Lisa, Manuel, 25
Los Angeles, Calif., 64

Magoffin, Susan, 39
Manco Burro Pass, 53, 142n. 34
Mangas Colorado, 82
Manifest Destiny, 49, 141n. 22
Martinez, Padre José Antonio, 48
Maxwell Land Grant. *See* Beaubien and Miranda Grant
Maxwell Land Grant and Railway Company, 105, 120–21, 129, 130
Maxwell Land Grant Company, 129, 131, 133
Maxwell, Deluvina, 89, 132
Maxwell, Emilia, 68, 105, 114
Maxwell, Father James (great-uncle of LM), 22
Maxwell, Ferdinand (brother of LM), 33, 98
Maxwell, Hugh (father of LM), 22, 26
Maxwell, Julian (adopted son of LM), 128
Maxwell, Lucien: with Carlos Beaubien, 41, 69; beaver hunt (last one), 63; Bent heirs' claim, 85; birth, 22; with Kit Carson, 35, 41, 49, 54, 61, 63; childhood amusements, 32; choice of advisors, 124; Cimarron residence, 75, 76, 79, 89, 92; death, 126; early years at Bent's Fort, 35, 40; family background, 25, 26, 31; family visits Kaskaskia, 69, 70; father's death, 33; First National Bank of Santa Fe, 112-13; Fort Sumner property ownership, 114, 147n. 19; Fort Sumner residence, 107, 113–14, 116; with Frémont, 41–42, 49, 50, 53–54, 118; gambling, 115; gold on the grant, 86–87, 97, 100; leadership style, 71, 80, 93; Los Angeles visit, 64; Manco Burro Pass, 53; marriage, 41; Mother's death, 83; New York City visit, 104; with Penitentes, 95; probate court judge, 99; purchase of BM Grant, 68, 69, 84–

85, 97, 100, 102; railroad investment, 117, 147n. 34; Rayado residence, 54, 55, 60-62, 68; reconciliation with Virginia, 147n. 20; reported dead, 67; sale of Cimarron property, 105, 146nn. 8,9; sale of the grant, 100, 103–5, 122; Sangre de Cristo Grant, 69, 84; school, 33–34, 38; sheep to California, 63, 143n. 13; surgery at Fort Union, 91; Taos uprising, 50, 52
Maxwell, Luz Beaubien, 83, 109; and BM Grant, 74; 100, 103, 105; birth of first child, 52; at Cimarron, 75; death, 128, 132; at Fort Sumner, 107, 114, 127, 131; grandchildren, 104; Kaskaskia visit, 70; marriage, 41; Rayado, 60; Taos uprising, 51
Maxwell, Maria, 68, 70
Maxwell, Odile, 105, 115, 126, 128, 133, 135
Maxwell, Odile Menard (mother of LM), 22, 83
Maxwell, Paula (Paulita), 105, 115, 133
Maxwell, Peter, 52, 60, 68, 113
Maxwell, Sofia, 68, 105
Maxwell, Verenisa, 78, 83, 136
Maxwell, Virginia (Mrs. A.S.B. Keyes), 60, 68, 114; Arizona story, 133; death, 132; marriage to A.S.B. Keyes, 103; reconciliation with LM, 104, 114, 146n. 9, 147n. 20
McMains, Rev. Oscar P., 128
Medicine Lodge Treaty, 98
Memphis and El Paso Railroad, 118
Menard, Michel Branamour, 22, 32-33, 62
Menard, Pierre, 22-26, 28, 32, 38, 131
Mexican Colonization Law of 1828, 48, 66
Mexican Land Grants, 46-48, 76, 108, 121-23
Mexican War, 48-50, 52, 54
Miller, Manuel (great-grandson of LM), 135
Miller, Stella (granddaughter of LM), 135
Mills, Melvin, 93, 111, 129
Miranda, Guadalupe, 47, 68
Miranda, Pablo, 97
Mississippi River, 21, 24, 30, 32, 69, 131
Missouri Fur Company, 23, 34
Missouri River, 21, 36, 69, 70
Monroe, James, 18
Mora, N.Mex., 99, 112
Moreno Water and Mining Company, 97
Morley (Cleaveland), Agnes, 96

Navajo Indians, 53, 81–83, 88, 98
Nevada, 70, 71
New York City, N.Y., 57, 104, 118
Norton, A.B., 17, 87, 89, 144n. 19

Owens, Dick, 53

Pecos River, 82, 88, 114, 116, 117, 136
Pelham, William, 68, 123
Penitentes, 95
Phillips, Waite, 133
Philmont Scout Ranch, 133
Polk, James K., 49, 54

Quinn, James, 52

Raton Pass, 51, 54, 100; A,T, SF RR, 24;
    Kearny's march through, 49; and
    Santa Fe Trail, 47, 59, 79; Wootton's
    toll road, 92
Raton, N.Mex., 131
Rayado, N.Mex., 52, 55, 60–62, 67, 68;
    house still stands, 136; permanent
    residence begins, 54; title to LM, 69
Rendezvous, 35, 37
Romero, Vicente, 96

Saint Louis, Mo., 21, 23, 25, 37, 41
Saint Mary's of the Barrens, 33–34, 38,
    51, 85, 127
Sainte Genevieve, Mo., 21, 22, 25, 32
San Francisco, Calif., 54, 64
Sand Creek, Colo., 83
Sangre de Cristo Grant, 48, 122, 123,
    137; confirmation, 68, 129; LM's
    interest in, 69, 84; sale to William
    Gilpin, 84
Sangre de Cristo Mountains, 47, 54, 59,
    76, 126
Santa Fe Ring, 101, 113, 124, 129
Santa Fe Trail, 36, 41, 43, 48, 115;
    Becknell begins, 24; boundary BM
    Grant, 47; Chavez murder, 49; ends,
    119, 131, 135; Kearny's march, 49;
    LM's home on, 59, 68, 78-79; map, 13
Santa Fe, N.Mex., 24, 33, 36, 49, 80, 131
Sibley, George, 25, 47
Silva, Frank, 136
Silva, Jesús, 61, 114, 136
Smith, Joel Heflin, 133
Southern Pacific Railroad, 118
Springer, Frank, 129, 132

St. Vrain, Ceran, 35, 36, 39, 99; death,
    112; ends relationship with Bent, 58;
    Taos uprising, 51
Steck, Michael, 89
Sublette, William, 35

Taos uprising, 50–52
Taos, N.Mex., 24, 36, 41, 44, 47, 51, 60
Taylor, Zachary, 56
Texas, 43, 47, 49, 118; Menards in
    Galveston, 22, 33, 62; statehood, 56
Tolby, Rev. T.J., 128
Treaty of Guadalupe Hidalgo, 52, 66,123

Ute Indians, 24, 36, 53, 60, 62; at
    Cimarron, 82, 85, 88, 99, 112, 125–26;
    removal to reservation, 128, 130;
    Treaty 1846, 66; Treaty 1849, 66;
    Treaty 1868, 98

Vincentians, 34, 85, 94, 126

Walker, William, 94
Watrous, Samuel, 96
Watts, John S., 104, 113, 121
Welborn, Adelina, 94, 133
Westphall, Victor: LM's ownership of
    Fort Sumner land, 114, 147n. 19;
    perimeters of Beaubien Miranda
    Grant, 47, 122
Wootton, Dick, 63, 71, 92

Young, Brigham, 56